Routledge Revivals

The Construction Industry in Developing Countries

The Construction Industry in Developing Countries (1986) examines this vital form of economic activity, often the second-largest employer after agriculture in the developing world. The construction industry is not just a key source of employment, but is also a dynamic factor in the process of economic growth and development.

The Construction Industry in Developing Countries

Alternative Strategies for Development

Jill Wells

Routledge
Taylor & Francis Group

First published in 1986
by Croom Helm Ltd

This edition first published in 2026 by Routledge
4 Park Square, Milton Park, Abingdon, Oxon, OX14 4RN

and by Routledge
605 Third Avenue, New York, NY 10017

Routledge is an imprint of the Taylor & Francis Group, an informa business

Publisher's Note
The publisher has gone to great lengths to ensure the quality of this reprint but points out that some imperfections in the original copies may be apparent.

Disclaimer
The publisher has made every effort to trace copyright holders and welcomes correspondence from those they have been unable to contact.

A Library of Congress record exists under LCCN: 86011672

ISBN: 978-1-041-29725-3 (hbk)
ISBN: 978-1-003-77093-0 (ebk)
ISBN: 978-1-041-29728-4 (pbk)

Book DOI 10.4324/9781003770930

THE CONSTRUCTION INDUSTRY IN DEVELOPING COUNTRIES:

ALTERNATIVE STRATEGIES FOR DEVELOPMENT

JILL WELLS

CROOM HELM
London • Sydney • Dover, New Hampshire

Croom Helm Ltd, Provident House, Burrell Row,
Beckenham, Kent, BR3 1AT

Croom Helm Australia Pty Ltd, Suite 4, 6th Floor,
64-76 Kippax Street, Surry Hills, NSW 2010, Australia

British Library Cataloguing in Publication Data

Wells, Jill

The construction industry in developing
countries: alternative strategies for
development.
1. Construction industry — Developing
countries
I. Title
338.4'7624'091724 HD9715.D42

ISBN 0-7099-3626-5

Croom Helm, 27 South Main Street,
Wolfeboro, New Hampshire 03894-2069, USA

Library of Congress Cataloging-in-Publication Data

Wells, Jill,

The construction industry in developing countries.

Bibliography: p.
1. Construction industry – Developing countries.
I. Title.
HD9715.D44W45 1986 338.4'7624'091724 86-11672
ISBN 0-7099-3626-5

Printed and bound in Great Britain
by Billing & Sons Limited, Worcester.

CONTENTS

TABLES AND FIGURES

Tables

Figures

For my husband, James Turner, who gave so much that this book might be written, but did not live to see it completed

Preface

Construction is a vital form of economic activity. In the industrialised countries value-added in construction commonly accounts for some seven per cent of Gross Domestic Product (GDP). As a large percentage of inputs to the sector are 'bought-in' from other sectors of the economy (notably the building materials industries) gross output may be double this figure. As much as ten per cent of the labour force is commonly employed in the construction and building materials industries, which may in fact be the biggest employer of any single industry or service sector.

In poorer and less-developed countries the construction sector appears at first sight to occupy a less important place within the economy as a whole. Thus value-added in construction in Tanzania in 1983 amounted to only 3.8 per cent of GDP; in Kenya it was five per cent. It must be remembered, however, that in these countries the manufacturing sector also is little-developed. So that construction may still be the largest single employer outside of agriculture. Also it should be noted that much of the construction activity that takes place in countries such as Kenya and Tanzania is of a kind that is simply not counted in official statistics - traditional construction around the fringes of the monetary economy.

Even more important than the place of construction in the economy at any one point in time is the fact that construction activity plays a dynamic role in the process of economic growth and development. This is because the final products of the sector (roads, harbours, factories, offices, hospitals, schools and houses) are all regarded as 'capital' or 'investment' goods. As such they are not consumed just for their own sake, but are actually used for the production of other goods, services or means of production. Thus construction is a major capital goods industry. In fact it is possible to argue that it is *the* major capital goods industry, as in most countries (both rich and poor) approximately one half of all investment in capital goods is in the products of this sector.

Yet despite the fact that the construction sector occupies an important place in the economy of all countries and plays a dynamic role in the process of growth and development, it is an industrial sector that is all too frequently ignored by economists, planners, administrators, politicians and others concerned with development issues. The development literature is full of books on agriculture, mining, manufacturing, transport, trade and services and yet there are few books on the subject of construction. There are even fewer that focus upon construction in developing countries, or venture into the uncharted territory of the complex relationships between construction activity and economic growth. Neither is construction afforded any special attention in more general texts. Even in books dealing specifically with industry, construction is rarely given a separate section and sometimes not even a mention. As a result, many people fail to grasp the concept of construction as a separate and identifiable economic sector. If it is considered at all, it is a subject that all too frequently seems to be shrouded in mystery.

The aim of this book is to 'de-mystify'; to shed light where there was previously only darkness. In reading the book the reasons for the ignorance of, and mystification surrounding, this vital sector should become apparent. The construction process is complicated by a number of factors quite specific to this branch of economic activity. But it is also unnecessarily and excessively complicated (and this is especially so in the very poor countries with which the book is most concerned) by outdated, inappropriate and irrational rules, regulations and procedures, embedded in the capitalist mode of production and inherited from former colonial powers. Thus, the way in which demand is organised, contracts let, and projects implemented inhibits the development of more cost-efficient designs for construction projects, using locally-available materials and locally-developed technologies. The fragmentation of demand and lack of continuity of production also inhibits fixed capital investment in the construction industry, and encourages producers to keep their assets mobile - hence restricting the development of local resources of materials and the training of local labour. It is only by recognising and understanding these contradictions and by critically examining, and if necessary discarding, outdated and irrelevant procedures and institutions in the construction sector, that more appropriate and more productive construction industries will be developed. It is hoped that this book will somehow help in the process.

In Chapter one some characteristics of construction activity are highlighted and the construction process in planned and in market economies described. Chapter two examines further the role of construction in the economy, and in economic development, and outlines the benefits to be gained from the existence of a strong indigenous construction capacity. The fact that a number of countries are very far from achieving this objective is shown in Chapter three, which describes the poverty of resources in the construction sector in East Africa and elsewhere. Before resources can be developed, a number of barriers within the structure of the construction industry must be removed; these impediments to the full development of productive resources are analysed and explained in Chapter four. Proposals for a solution are explored in Chapter five. Since actual policies adopted in any country will depend upon local circumstances, the development strategy adopted and the authority which the state is in practice able to command, there can be no 'blue-print' for development. As an alternative an attempt is therefore made in Part two to examine the progress to-date in developing construction resources in three small countries - Kenya, Tanzania and Cuba; countries with very different political objectives, economic systems and strategies for development.

ACKNOWLEDGEMENTS

Thanks are due to Andrew Coulson, Chris Gerry and Paul Strassmann for their constructive criticisms of the first draft of the manuscript. For help of various different kinds, over a number of years, I am deeply indebted to Yngve Palm of the UN/ECE, Emanuel Csorba of UNIDO, and Mario Piche of UNCHS; in Kenya to David Mutiso, Bill Campbell, Onesimus Gichuiri and Sam Muturi; in Tanzania to Cleopa Msuya, George Mlingwa, R. Balasuperamanium and Nes Lemunge; and in Cuba to Emilio Escobar. At home in Wales, my biggest debt is to David and Do Burgess; to the management and staff of E. Turner & Sons Ltd. (building contractors); and last but not least to my daughter, Lisa, for spending so many holidays in uncomfortable situations.

PART ONE

ASPECTS OF THE CONSTRUCTION INDUSTRY IN DEVELOPING COUNTRIES

Chapter One

INTRODUCTION

SOME CHARACTERISTICS OF CONSTRUCTION

The products of the construction sector differ widely in terms of size, appearance, location and in terms of end-use. In many of the least developed countries in the world today as much as one half of the total construction output may be in civil-engineering projects (roads, railways, ports, dams, power stations, drainage projects or water supplies) forming the basic infrastructure that is so vital to all other forms of economic and social activity. Commercially-built housing is generally less than one-third of the total. The remainder of new construction work is in the form of other buildings (hospitals, health centres, schools, offices, factories, agricultural buildings and hotels). Also included in data for net output, or value-added, by the construction sector is the on-going repair and maintenance of all existing structures - a frequently much-neglected form of economic activity in the poorer countries, but one which is now beginning to receive some of the attention it deserves.

The products of the construction industry also show wide variations in terms of the materials and techniques used in production and the standards (in terms of space, quality and durability, as well as aesthetic considerations) of the finished product. So that within the category of 'roads' may be included a fully-bitumenised, six-lane motorway, as well as a single-lane dirt track. Within the single category of 'housing' is grouped a detached villa constructed to a high standard with permanent materials, a modern high-rise apartment block, constructed in cement and steel with the aid of a tower crane and a simple house of mud or bamboo, maybe with a soil-cement floor and corrugated iron roof. Within the construction sector there in fact exists considerable scope for substitution between inputs and a high degree of technological flexibility in production. In the poorest countries, the full range of technological alternatives is generally adopted (although, it may be argued, not always in the right way) and is indeed very clearly visible upon the landscape.

The heterogeneous nature of the products of the industry - in terms of inputs, technology, standards and end-use - is perhaps part of the explanation for the widespread failure of economists and others concerned with development issues (not to mention the public at large) to grasp the concept of construction as a clearly identifiable economic sector in its own right. The heterogeneity of the products and particularly the great variety of end-uses to which they are put, are also frequently held to account for the fact that construction is 'different' from other economic sectors. Thus it is argued that there is not, and cannot be, any such thing as a standard construction product. A house is not, and cannot be, the same product as a hospital or a school. And this variety of end-use inhibits the process of standardisation of construction products and thus reduces the prospects for continuous production runs of identical items, or 'mass-production'. For this reason, construction is commonly seen not as an industry at all but rather as an activity, or a collection of activities.

While there is undoubtedly some truth in the idea that construction is different from other forms of economic activity, it is important to understand these differences and to place them in a proper perspective. Thus whilst it is true that construction products serve a wide variety of functions, so in fact do the products of other industries, from textiles, to automobiles, to steel. The problem of variety of end-use in these industries is overcome by the maximum possible standardisation of the products and also by the standardisation and mass-production of the parts, or components, that make up the production of the finished article. This can happen to some extent in construction. So that even if a house is not the same commodity as a hospital or a school, there can be standard houses or standard schools. Even more significantly, there can be standard components for houses or schools, which may also serve as inputs to a wide variety of other buildings. The process of standardisation (of final products or of component parts) in the construction sector has in fact progressed a very long way in a number of countries - principally, but not exclusively, in the socialist or planned economies of the USSR and Eastern Europe.

A far more significant distinguishing characteristic of construction - perhaps its only truly unique feature - is the fact that the completed products are generally not mobile but fixed for all time in the particular location where they are built. Thus, even if parts of the structure may be manufactured elsewhere, the final assembly process is site-specific. This fact has two important implications. First, it places quite clear limits upon the process of centralised mass-production of component parts, or 'prefabrication'; for the economies that may be gained from mass-production must always be balanced against the subsequent costs of transporting component parts or sections of a structure to the construction site. As such parts are typically large and bulky items and of low value in relation to their weight the costs of transport will be substantial. In developing countries with poor communications, they are generally prohibitive. Secondly, the fact that construction products are site-specific, i.e. that they are produced where they are to be consumed and cannot afterwards be transported, means that in general the final products of the construction industry cannot be produced in advance of demand but rather have to be sold before they are produced, or made to order. There are a few notable exceptions to this general rule, such as speculative housing and offices in cities, or advance factories in special areas, where the demand for built space may be concentrated, continuous and predictable. But by and large the products of the construction industry are first planned, then ordered and finally produced at the particular location where they are required. Thus each product is in a very real sense unique. This means that while component parts for buildings may to some extent be produced on a continuous basis, and stockpiled when demand is slack, complete buildings, roads, dams or power stations may not. Continuity of production in the construction sector is therefore dependent upon the maintenance of continuity of demand.

Continuous demand is, however, something that the construction industry is largely denied. It has already been noted that a large part of the output of construction consists of capital goods - products required for the production of other goods. As a result of this fact, construction, in common with other capital goods industries, is in fact peculiarly susceptible to variations in the level of activity in the economy as a whole. Thus during periods of rapid economic expansion construction output is required to grow at a faster rate than that of other sectors and during periods of stagnation or decline the construction industry is the first to suffer. These, to some extent inevitable, fluctuations in demand tend to be exacerbated in many capitalist economies by the practice of governments using the construction sector as an economic regulator, cutting back on construction projects or funds for investment when the economy is overheating and deliberately stimulating investment during periods of unemployment and slack demand. Thus wide fluctuation in the level of demand are endemic to the construction industry, at least in unplanned, or market, economies. Given the difficulties of stockpiling products that have to be made to order, levels of output must also fluctuate accordingly.

CONSTRUCTION IN PLANNED ECONOMIES

The special characteristics of the construction industry, as outlined above (i.e. the heterogeneity of the products of the industry, the fact that they are tied to a particular location and have to be produced where they are to be consumed and the fact that levels of output are subject to wide fluctuations) are to some extent common to construction in all countries. In the socialist or planned economies, however, these special features of construction have been, if not entirely overcome, at least reduced in significance. Thus in the Soviet Union and the countries of Eastern Europe the production of buildings has been subjected to a process of 'rationalisation', whereby buildings are reduced to a number of common constituent parts, many of which can be 'prefabricated', or manufactured in long production runs, frequently away from the site in some central location. Such common parts, or standard components are then transported to different sites, and put together in a number of ways, to produce a variety of end products. Frequently referred to as 'industrialisation', or 'systems building', this kind of rationalisation of the building process requires a high degree of coordination of the demand for construction products, and a willingness to accept a certain degree of standardisation in the final structures. It also requires, for efficient operation, a certain continuity of production - a levelling of the peaks and troughs of construction demand, such as may be achieved (albeit imperfectly) in a planned economy through the process of planning itself. Thus in planned economies the construction process has been rationalised to a large extent and levels of output, if not stable, have at least been kept generally in line with the level of activity in the economy as a whole.

THE CONSTRUCTION PROCESS UNDER CAPITALISM

In the 'unplanned' or market economies on the other hand (including the vast majority of least developed economies) attempts at standardisation of the product and rationalisation of the building process have, with one or two notable exceptions, largely resulted in failure. Far from ironing out the peaks and troughs in demand, governments with their 'stop go' policies have helped to exaggerate them. The resulting discontinuity of production is exaggerated even further by the fact that demand is fragmented among a myriad of different bodies, or clients, of the construction industry and seldom are attempts made to coordinate or structure that demand in any sort of rational way. The particular industrial structure that has developed in construction under capitalism is largely a response to this situation.

The most obvious and striking feature of the construction industry in capitalist countries is the fact that the responsibility for production is divided among a wide variety of participants. The major participants may include any, or all, of the following: the client, who commissions the structure but may or may not be the ultimate user; the construction professionals (architects and engineers) who design the project; sometimes a quantity surveyor who measures from the drawings in order to arrive at an estimated price; a main contractor who undertakes the major part of the responsibility for the actual construction; various subcontractors, either specialised in various trades or in the business of providing 'labour only', to whom responsibility for minor parts of the construction work may be assigned; the producers and suppliers of building materials, plant, equipment and utilities;

as well as suppliers of finance, transport, insurance and various other subsidiary services.

While with the increasing complexity of modern structures one would expect to see some degree of specialisation in the various aspects of the construction process, what is somewhat surprising is the particular way in which such specialisation has developed in the construction industry. Even more surprising is the fact that the various specialists not only perform separate functions but that they also belong to quite separate commercial organisations, with quite different structures, objectives and methods of remunreration - the relations between which are essentially hierarchical and all too frequently adversarial rather than cooperative. There are in fact many variations of contractual arrangements, rules and regulations governing the relationships between the various organisations, and their participants, in the construction process. But the most usual pattern is as follows:

1. The potential owner, or the client, first selects his professional team (architects and engineers, who may be either from the same or different firms), gives them an idea of what he requires and what he is prepared to pay.
2. The architect or engineer produces a preliminary design, and brings in whatever other specialist professional services that may be required (structural, electrical or mechanical engineers etc.) for completion of the detailed design.
3. After designs have been agreed and more or less completed, the project is put out to competitive tender - either in the form of a 'lump sum' contract (usually for very small works) based upon the drawings and specification alone, or on the basis of a 'bill of quantities' prepared by an independent firm of quantity surveyors.
4. The construction firm submitting the lowest tender is generally awarded the contract, and subsequently known as the 'main contractor'; he undertakes to complete the construction for the stated price, or in the case of a re-measured contract, according to the bill of quantity rates.

5. The main contractor may subcontract part (or sometimes all) of the work to various subcontractors; and certain parts of the work may be carried out by subcontractors nominated by the architect or engineer. But the main contractor carries the financial risks involved in construction, and takes as his reward any profit he might make.
6. By contrast, the professionals - architects, engineers and surveyors - are rewarded for their services in the form of a fee, normally calculated as a fixed percentage of the final cost of the contract.

This brief outline obviously overlooks a number of important details, and ignores all of the possible variations that exist in the relations between the various participants in the construction industry. Thus it is not the only way of executing construction projects, but it is still the most common way in the developing countries with which we are concerned. It is therefore worthwhile noting briefly at this stage, some of the more significant features of the system.

Most immediately apparent is the fact that the responsibility for the design of construction projects is completely divorced from the responsibility for their production. Furthermore, this separation has been accompanied by quite significant professional, legal and institutional barriers to cooperation between designers and producers in the construction industry - which has serious, and fairly obvious, negative implications for the efficiency of the total construction process. This will be dealt with at some length in Chapter four. Of equal, but perhaps less obvious, significance is the fact that under this system of building by contract, firms in the main business of construction are forced to compete for each and every contract, on the basis of a given design, after it is put out to tender by the client or his professional advisers. This means that contractors undertake contracts on a purely 'one-off' basis, with no knowledge or foresight of their future work-load, and thus no ability to plan ahead or to invest for the future. Consequently, it is in their interests to make only the minimum of investments in fixed capital, to take on only the minimum of permanent staff, while maximising their use of subcontracting and casual labour.

It is easy to see that the extreme fragmentation of the construction industry (with participation by a large number of separate commercial entities, each keeping its assets highly mobile and relating to each other by means of contracts) is in large part a response to uncertainty, to the problem of discontinuous production and fragmented demand in the construction sector. It is a good response, in so far as it provides for a high degree of mobility of resources within the industry, and a great deal of flexibility in their use. But there is a price to be paid. For extensive reliance upon the use of subcontracting and casual labour, and a reluctance to invest in fixed capital assets, both have serious implications for the productivity of the construction industry as a whole - and this is particularly so in countries where construction resources are seriously underdeveloped. At the same time, the absence of effective planning and the existence of a number of strong vested interests among the independent construction professions, serve to obstruct any movement towards a greater degree of standardisation of either construction products or components. In fact it is the thesis of this book that the particular industrial structure that has been adopted hampers the development of productive resources in the construction sector of developing countries and obviates the adoption of a more appropriate construction technology based upon local resources. Before developing the argument further in chapter four it is necessary first to look at the overall significance of construction to development (chapter two) and the present degree of poverty of construction resources in a number of developing countries (chapter three).

Chapter Two

CONSTRUCTION AND ECONOMIC GROWTH

The fragmentation of the construction industry, as described in the last chapter, leads to difficulties in the definition of its boundaries. The boundaries of construction are in fact frequently drawn very narrowly, to include only the main contractor. But while it is true that the main contractor plays a vital role in the construction process, he is not responsible for the whole of it. Two crucially important aspects - the design of the products and the production of materials and components - are generally excluded from his area of control. Since there is no logical separation of design from production in the construction process, it would be equally illogical to exclude the vital process of design from any definition or consideration of construction. Similarly, the interface between the construction and the building materials industries is never hard and fast, but essentially fluctuating and mobile - as between countries or within any one country over time; in the planned economies, with their far greater reliance upon prefabrication, it tends to disappear altogether.[1] Thus building materials production, even when carried out by separate organisations and classified under separate industrial headings, is an essential part of the process of construction and should be recognised as such - although in practice this may be difficult as some firms produce glass, ceramics, metal, wooden and chemical products for both construction and other uses.

It should also be noted that the contracting industry, although obviously important in many countries, is not necessarily the only means of execution of construction projects. In all countries, both developed and developing, central governments, local authorities, parastatal and/or voluntary organisations may have their own 'direct works' units for the execution of construction projects (both new works and repairs and maintenance) by 'force account'.[2] In many countries such bodies also have their own capacity for design and for the production of building materials. In addition, in a number of countries there are state-owned contracting organisations, such as national housing corporations or national construction companies, who may undertake a variety of types of construction work. The significance of such public-sector construction organisations in the implementation of government building programmes obviously varies, but in many of the smallest and poorest countries (with which this book is most concerned) they undertake practically all maintenance and repair work in the public sector, and a substantial amount of new work as well. They are also the main source of trained personnel for the construction industry at large - and hence assume an even greater significance than the volume of work carried out might imply.

Neither can it be overlooked that a large amount of construction work in developing countries is not executed within the 'formal sector' of the construction industry at all, but takes place in the informal sector, on the fringes of the monetary economy. Interpretations and definitions of the informal sector vary widely.[3] For purposes of the present study the informal construction sector will be understood to embrace all of those individuals or enterprises engaged in 'unenumerated' or 'unregulated' construction activity, including (but not restricted to) the self-help construction activities of slum and squatter residents.[4] It does not include any enterprises engaging in construction work undertaken with official planning approval, or that carried out by officially recognised organisations, such as contractors.

Thus it can be seen that there are many vital construction processes - both main and ancillary activities - that are not carried out by contractors; and this is especially true in developing countries. The contracting industry is *not* synonymous with the construction industry - although many continue to assume that it is.[5] In fact, by focusing on the contracting business it becomes all too easy to neglect other parts of the construction process, and other aspects of the construction industry. Even more important, it obviates the possibility of examining alternative ways of organising resources in this vital field, which is the major purpose of the present study. The construction industry will therefore be defined to include not just the activities generally carried out by main contractors but rather the whole construction process, including the production of building materials and the processes of planning and design, in both the public and private, formal and informal, sectors.

THE PLACE OF CONSTRUCTION IN THE ECONOMY

Assessment of the total value of construction output in any economy is beset with difficulties. In spite of the fact that construction appears twice in the national accounts of most countries (the only sector so to do), nowhere in the national accounts of any country is there a comprehensive picture of the total output of construction. This is firstly because the value-added by construction to the GDP (Gross Domestic Product) is the difference between the value of sales at market prices and the market value of all current purchases, and therefore excludes the value of purchased building materials and components, fuel, transport, professional services, insurance and legal fees.[6] On the other hand, while capital formation in construction *is* a measure of the gross output of the construction sector, and therefore does include the value of goods and services supplied to the construction industry from other sectors, it unfortunately excludes that which is not considered to accrue to the formation of new capital - which is much of repairs and maintenance work, amounting to as much as one third of the total output of the sector.

In most developing countries, the problem is compounded by the fact that a large percentage of construction activity is not executed within the formal sector of the construction industry but takes place in the 'informal sector', sometimes by self-help or unpaid labour. It is therefore frequently omitted altogether from national statistics or, if it is included, the methods of assessment are of necessity crude.[7] In addition, construction activity in developing countries is subject to wide fluctuations from year to year, and indeed from month to month; due to the casual nature of much construction employment, these figures fluctuate even more. And finally, despite the efforts of international organisations to bring consistency in the definition and presentation of national statistics, considerable deviation from the standardised systems remain in the data of many countries. Thus all data relating to

Table 2.1: The Contribution of Construction to GDP, GFCF and Employment in Selected Countries.

Country	(1) Per cap. GDP (U.S. Dollars)	(2) Net Constr. % of GDP (1977/79)	(3) Gross Constr. % of GDP (1978)	(4) Employment % of EAP	(5) Constr. % of GFCF (1978)
Ethiopia	97 (75)	4 (74/86)	6.9	-	66
Bangladesh	114	5	-	0.2 (74)	-
Nepal	121	7	12.3	0.1 (76)	73.7
Lesotho	124 (75)	2 (64/74)	7.5	-	76
Upper Volta	126	4 (74)	12.1	-	46
Burma	133	1	-	1.4 (77/78)	-
Burundi	146	4	-	-	-
Niger	160 (75)	3 (69)	-	-	-
Zaire	172 (77)	4 (77)	11.3	-	38
Chad	172 (75)	3 (75)	-	-	-
Malawi	178	4 (72/73)	8.0	2.1 (77)	42
India	187	5	9.6	1.2 (71)	54
Rwanda	194	3	-	-	-
Sri Lanka	196	5	7.5	3.8 (80)	42
Afghanistan	200 (75)	3 (74/76)	-	1.3 (79)	-
C.A.R.	200 (75)	4 (70)	-	-	-
Yemen	215 (75)	3 (72/73)	8.0	4.7 (75)	78
Benin	221	4	-	-	-
Uganda	222 (75)	1 (74/76)	8.0	-	49
Tanzania	249	3	5.8	0.5 (67)	32

Madagascar	253	3 (72/74)	-	-	-
Pakistan	254	5	10.2	4.1 (78)	62.7
Sierra Leone	283	3 (77/78)	8.2	-	65
Indonesia	350	6	-	1.5 (78)	-
Mauritania	353	4 (78)	-	-	-
Togo	353	7	-	-	-
Kenya	359	5	10.4	-	43
Senegal	361	4	-	-	-
Liberia	427	6 (76/78)	-	0.9 (74)	-
Tonga	464	4	-	5.4 (76)	-
Dominica	484	5	12.5	-	33
Sudan	488 (77)	4 (76/77)	-	2.0 (73)	-
Zambia	495	5	15.5	4.4 (69)	59 (73)
Thailand	512	5	10.75	1.5 (78)	43.7
Honduras	529	5	11.0 (75)	3.3 (77)	56 (76)
Phillipines	536	7	11.2	3.3 (77)	50.9
Guyana	540 (77)	7 (75/76)	-	6.2 (77)	-
Zimbabwe	592	3	7.9 (77)	-	58 (77)
Cameroon	612	4 (76)	11.2	1.7 (76)	54
Egypt	628	5	-	3.5 (77)	-
Morocco	657	8 (76/77)	-	4.3 (71)	-
Peru	657	3	6.3	4.2 (82)	56.6
Papua-New Guinea	662	7 (74/76)	-	-	-
El Salvador	684	5	9.1 (75)	5.4 (78)	39.5 (75)
Iran	2209 (77)	9	-	12.3 (76)	-
Venezuela	3035	7	21.4	8.8 (77)	51.2
Hong Kong	3140	7	11.8	7.8 (80)	53.6
Singapore	3328	6	9.5	5.2 (78)	32
Greece	3377	8	12.8	8.3 (77)	63
Ireland	3636	8 (75/76)	14.5	7.5 (77)	52.9

Table 2.1 (cont'd)

Country	(1) Per cap. GDP (U.S. Dollars)	(2) Net Constr. % of GDP (1977/79)	(3) Gross Constr. % of GDP (1978)	(4) Employment % of EAP	(5) Constr. % of GFCF (1978)
Puerto Rico	3707	3	7.8	7.7 (79)	57.7
Israel	3948	9	12.2	6.6 (78)	57.5
Spain	4019	8	12.5	8.7 (78)	56.7 (76)
Gabon	4425	10	-	-	-
Italy	4620	7	-	9.3 (78)	-
New Zealand	4838	5	12.1	8.8 (76)	59.8
U.K.	5624	6	8.8	6.3 (77)	48.9
Finland	7155	7	16	8.5 (76)	67
(Libya)	7262	10.5	-	16.4 (73)	-
Austria	7670	8	14.5	9.3 (78)	55
Australia	8116	7	12.3	7.1 (76)	56
Japan	8381	9	21	9.4 (78)	64
Canada	8720	6	13.2	5.9 (79)	61.5
France	8903	7	-	8.3 (78)	-
(Saudi Arabia)	9284	14	-	-	79.7
Netherlands	9337	7	12.3	10.9 (79)	57.7
Luxembourg	9723	10	14	9.1 (70)	60
USA	9748	5	10.9	6.2 (77)	56.5
Belgium	9855	8	14.4	7.3 (78)	68
Norway	10012	8	20.4	8.6 (78)	68.4
Germany	10444	7	12.8	7.2 (78)	57
Sweden	10934	7	11.4	6.9 (78)	60
Denmark	11168	9	13.3	8.0 (78)	60.5
(Kuwait)	12711	4	-	20.0 (80)	-

(U.A.E.)	19380	10	-	31.7 (75)	-

Note: countries in brackets have been excluded from calculations of averages for the countries in this group.

Swaziland	707 (75)	2 (74/76)	3.9	-	-
Nigeria	717 (77)	9 (77)	18.5	-	63.8
Belize	757	6 (73/76)	10.9	-	38.0
Bolivia	762	5	8.2	5.5 (76)	46.0
Botswana	830	5	17.8	-	59.8
Jordan	865	6	22.3	13.6 (79)	56.0
Paraguay	886	5	13.2	4.5 (81)	51.7
Nicaragua	889	4 (77/78)	5.4	4.8 (77)	37.9
Ghana	913 (77)	4 (76/77)	8.9	-	66.8
Columbia	914	4	9.3	2.9 (80)	50.0
Dominican Repub.	918	7	13.5	2.3 (70)	61.0
Equador	968	7	11.8	4.7 (80)	48.0
Tunisia	981	7	15.6	8.6 (75)	58.9
Lebanon	989	3 (77)	-	-	-
Mauritius	1012	8	23.0	8.2 (72)	66.8
Ivory Coast	1014	7	19.2	-	63
Syria	1030	5	15.6	12.0 (78)	53.8
Malaysia	1045 (77)	4 (73)	-	4.9 (79)	-
Chile	1078 (77)	2	4.3	5.2 (80)	44.3 (76)
Turkey	1161	5	13.7	4.2 (80)	61 (77)
South Korea	1285	8	17.6	5.9 (78)	47
Panama	1343	6	13.7	6.1 (79)	59
Algeria	1344	12 (73/76)	26.9	10.2 (77)	59 (76)
Mexico	1393	6	11.9	4.6 (79)	54
Argentina	1448 (75)	4	12.4	-	59 (75)
Iraq	1604	2 (74/75)	15.5	10.3 (77)	58

Table 2.1 (cont'd).

Country	Per cap. GDP (U.S. Dollars)	Net Constr. % of GDP (1977/79)	Gross Constr. % of GDP (1978)	Employment % of EAP	Constr. % of GFCF (1978)
South Africa	1611	4	12.8	5.6 (70)	51
Costa Rica	1654	6	-	7.9 (80)	-
Brazil	1675	5	-	6.7 (76)	-
Uruguay	1731	4	12.3	-	64.5
Portugal	1816	5 (75/76)	8.8	7.9 (78)	62.7

Source: U.N. Yearbook of National Account Statistics: ILO Yearbook of Labour Statistics.

the construction sector, especially in less developed countries, must be interpreted with caution.

Notwithstanding the above provisos, data on the contribution of construction sector output to GDP and to capital formation is available for a large number of countries in the United Nations Yearbook of National Account Statistics. Data on employment in construction can be found in the International Labour Office's Yearbook of Labour Statistics. Data drawn from these sources for over 100 countries is presented in Table 2.1. The table shows the following variables for each country: (1) GDP per capita; (2) value-added in construction as a percentage of GDP; (3) capital formation in construction (gross output) as a percentage of GDP; (4) employment in construction as a percentage of the EAP (Economically Active Population); and (5) investment in construction as a percentage of GFCF (Gross Fixed Capital Formation). In each case the GDP per capita and other figures included in the table are for the year 1978, or the most recent year for which data was available. In some instances an attempt has been made to obtain, for some variables, an average figure over three consecutive years (1977, 1978 and 1979, unless otherwise indicated). The countries in the table have been ranked in ascending order of per capita GDP.

A cursory glance at the data included in Table 2.1 reveals that value-added in construction as a percentage of GDP varies widely between countries - ranging from a low of only 1 per cent in Uganda and Burma, to highs of 12 per cent in Algeria and 14 per cent in Saudi Arabia. A similarly wide range may be found in the figures for gross output in construction (from 6 per cent to 26 per cent of GDP) and for construction employment (between 0.1 per cent of the EAP in Nepal and 16 per cent in Libya). Closer examination, however, reveals an underlying trend towards higher figures for construction output (as measured by the three variables) with increasing per capita GDP. Statistical analysis of the data in fact reveals a clear positive relationship between GDP per capita, and the three separate measures of construction activity - value-added as a percentage of GDP, gross output as a percentage of GDP and employment as a percentage of the EAP. This is illustrated in figures 2.1, 2.2 and 2.3 - where the solid line indicates the statistical relationship between the variables.[8]

Figure 2.1: The Relationship between Value-Added in Construction and Per Capita GDP.

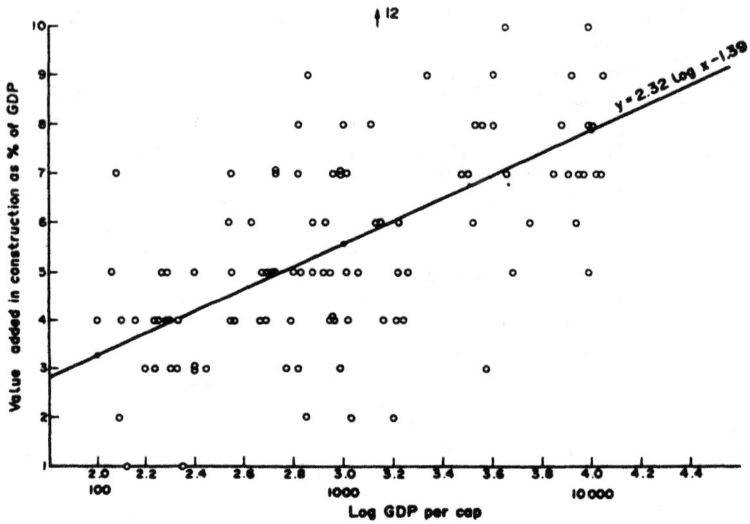

The pattern presented by the data, and the implications, can be more clearly understood if countries are divided into groups according to per capita GDP, and average values calculated for each of the relevant variables within each group. The results of such an exercise are presented below, in Table 2.2. Thus, despite the apparently wide range within each group, value-added in construction was found to average only 3.6 per cent of GDP in the poorest group of countries; 5.2 per cent for countries in the next poorest group; 5.4 per cent for a middle-income group of countries; and around 7.3 per cent for countries with an average per capita income of above 2,000 dollars per annum. Similarly, employment in construction also increases from an average of 2.1 per cent of the EAP in Group I, to 3.4 per cent in Group II, 6.7 per cent in Group III and 8.1 per cent in Group IV.

Figure 2.2: The Relationship between Gross Construction Output and Per-Capita GDP

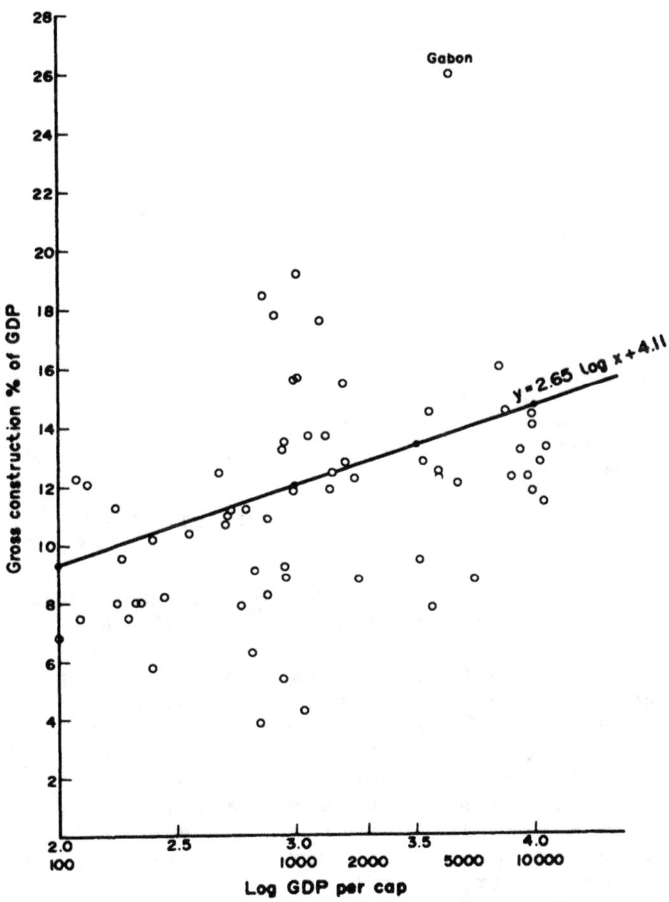

Figure 2.3: The Relationship between Employment in Construction and Per Capita GDP.

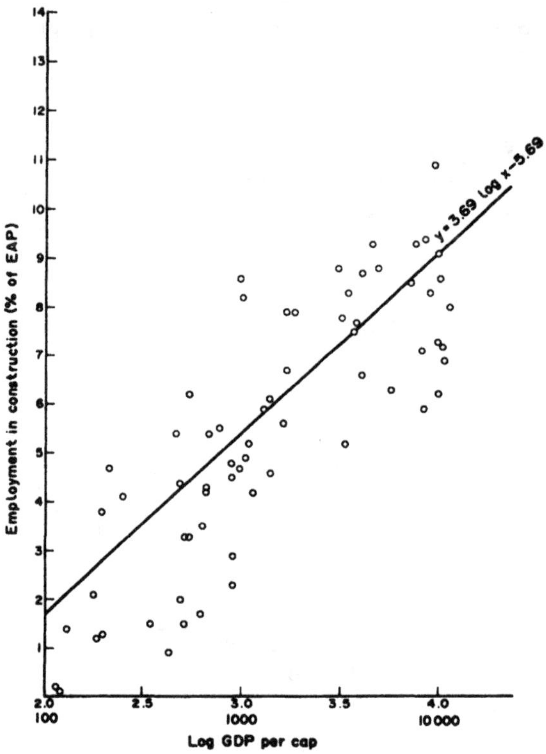

THE RELATIONSHIP BETWEEN CONSTRUCTION OUTPUT AND ECONOMIC GROWTH

The presentation and analysis of cross-section data drawn from a variety of countries, such as that presented above in Tables 2.1 and 2.2 and Figures 2.1, 2.2 and 2.3 is usually followed by an assumption that the relationships observed between countries at different income levels at a fixed point in time, also occur within any one country, over a period of time. If such an assumption were made, then on the basis of the above analysis one would expect construction output to represent an increasing share of GDP, with increasing per capita GDP, in any one country over time. To put it another way, as GDP increases construction output would grow at an even faster rate. Furthermore, one would expect the rate of growth of construction output to be fastest (the GDP elasticity of construction

Table 2.2: The Average Contribution of Construction to GDP, GFCF and Employment in Countries grouped according to Income

Variable	Group I Under US$350 *(per capita)*	Group II US$350-700	Group III US$700-2000	Group IV Over US$2,000
(1) Value added in construction as a % of GDP	3.6 (23)	5.2 (21)	5.4 (31)	7.3 (27)
(2) Capital formation in construction as a % of GDP	8.9 (13)	10.6 (10)	13.6 (27)	13.5 (23)
(3) Employment in construction as a % of EAP	3.1 (9)	3.4 (14)	6.6 (22)	8.1 (26)
(4) Construction as a % of GFCF	56 (13)	53 (10)	55.4 (26)	57.5 (23)

Note: Figures in brackets represent the number of countries included in each group

Source: Compiled from data in Table 2.1

to be greatest) as countries passed through the middle-income range, from 350 to 2000 dollars per capita GDP.

Commonsense tells us that this is a very plausible assumption. All products of the construction industry are regarded as investment goods, or a part of fixed capital formation. In fact the output of the construction sector constitutes a substantial proportion, on average more than one-half of Gross Fixed Capital Formation in all countries. As a high rate of investment (30 per cent of GDP is not uncommon) is essential for rapid economic growth and as construction constitutes around 50 per cent of that investment, it is therefore to be expected that whenever economic growth occurs it must be accompanied by a rapid increase in activity in the construction sector.

In order to test this hypothesis, average annual growth rates of construction output, of GDP and of manufacturing, for each group of countries included in the sample (i.e. multi-country averages over twenty years) have been calculated, and are shown in Table 2.3. It can be seen that the average growth rate of construction output has been positive for all groups of countries. For both the low and the middle-income groups, the growth rate of construction output has been greater than the growth rate of GDP. And undoubtedly the highest annual construction growth rates have occurred in the middle-income group where construction output has grown at an average annual rate of 8.6 per cent over twenty years - faster than both GDP and manufacturing.

Rapid growth in a number of countries - both market and centrally-planned economies - over the past 20 years presents an opportunity to make use of 'time-series data' to test further the central hypothesis that, during periods of rapid economic growth, construction output grows faster than national income and thus assumes an increasing percentage of GDP or NMP. Time-series data are not subject to the same limitations as cross-section data; they are also more interesting, reflecting actual events that have occurred in a particular country over time. Data have therefore been collected for a number of countries, all of which have experienced a period of rapid growth during the past two decades. The relationship over time between construction output and national income (GDP or NMP - Net Material Product), both expressed as index numbers reflecting output at constant prices, is shown for each of the countries separately in Figures

Table 2.3: Average Growth Rates of Construction and Manufacturing in Countries grouped according to Income.

	Group I (Under $350 per capita)	Group II ($350-700 per capita)	Group III ($700-2000 per capita)	Group IV (over $2000 per capita)
(1) Rate of growth of construction output (% per annum)	5.9	5.2	8.6	3.6
(2) Rate of growth of GDP	3.5	4.4	5.9	5.0
(3) Rate of growth of manufacturing	5.5	6.4	7.7	6.4
(4) No. of observations	(12)	(14)	(24)	(19)

Note: Growth rates are for the twenty year period, 1960-1979

Source: U.N. Yearbook of National Accounts Statistics

2.4 to 2.14. Construction output as a percentage of GDP or NMP is also shown. The first group of countries (Figs. 2.4 to 2.7) have seen rapid growth in the 1960s and 1970s mainly through the establishment of new industries; they are among the 'newly industrializing countries' or NICS. None of these countries has significant oil deposits. It must therefore be assumed that expansion of the construction sector has taken place in the absence of unlimited supplies of foreign-exchange. This is not the case with the second group of countries (Figs. 2.8 to 2.11), all of which are net exporters of oil, and in at least two of which (Nigeria and Saudi Arabia) it may be argued that oil discoveries have been the primary cause of rapid economic growth. The third group of countries (Figs. 2.12 and 2.14) consists of three centrally-planned economies (Yugoslavia), Romania and Cuba) which, although they may still be regarded as being among the less-developed countries, have all experienced significant expansion of their economies in recent years.

Although the actual rate of expansion of construction output and of national income differs among

Figures 2.4 to 2.7: The Relationship between Construction Output and GDP in Selected NICs.

Figure 2.4: South Korea

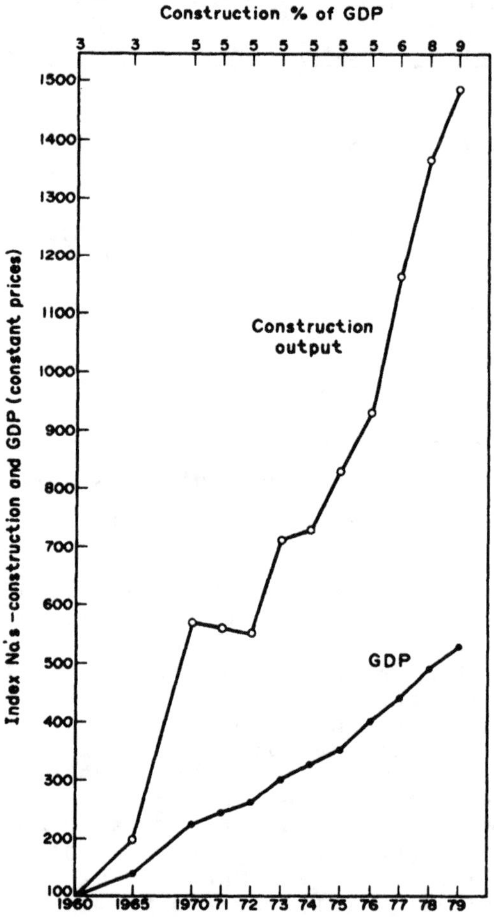

Figure 2.5: Singapore

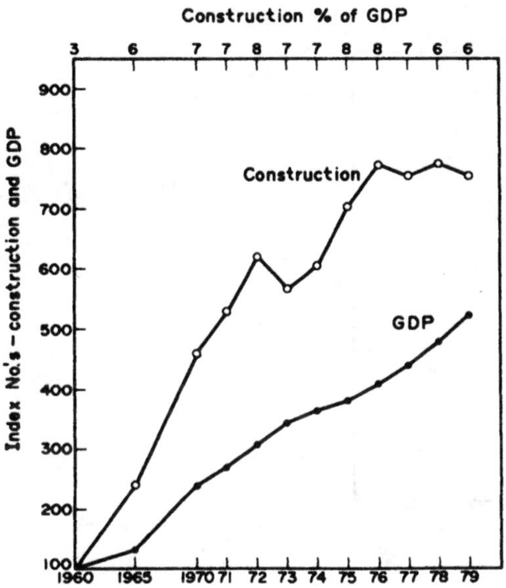

Figure 2.6: Philippines

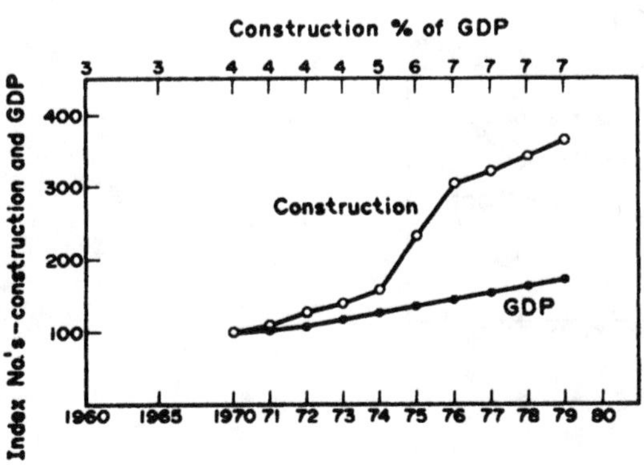

Figure 2.7: Morocco

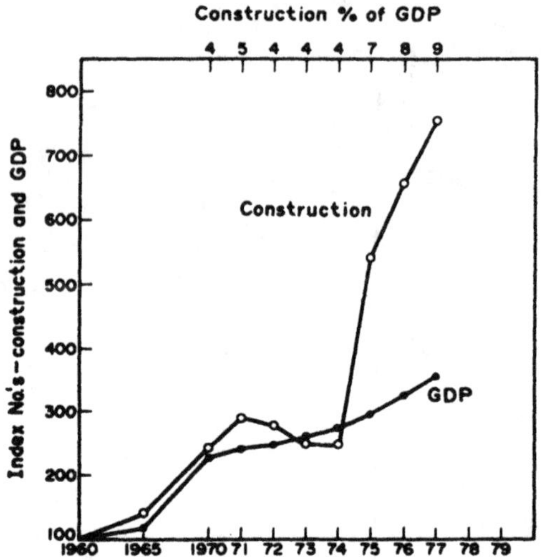

Figures 2.8 to 2.11: The Relationship between Construction Output and GDP in Oil-Exporting Countries

Figure 2.8: Mexico

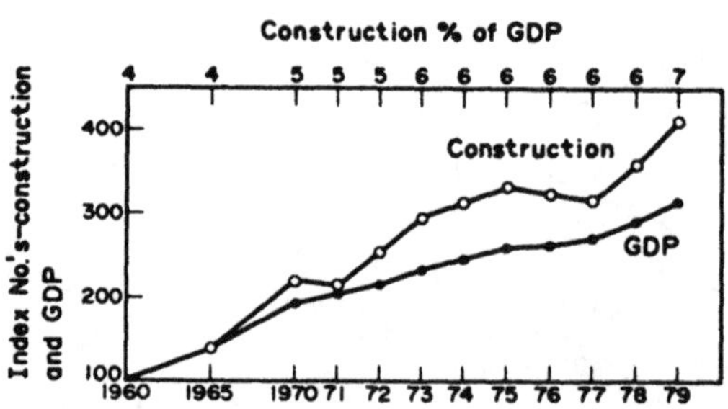

Figure 2.9: Equador

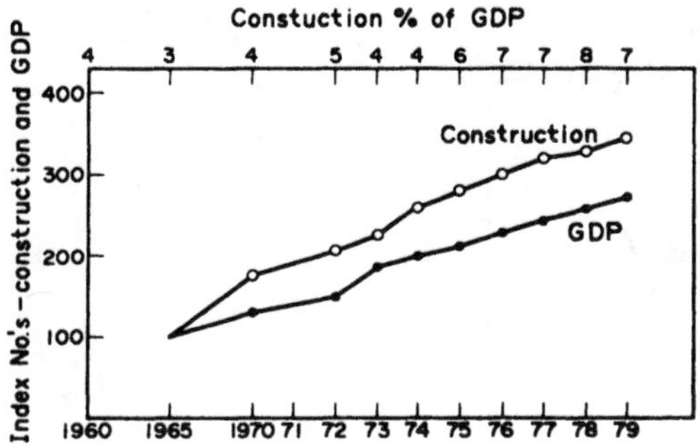

Figure 2.10: Saudi Arabia

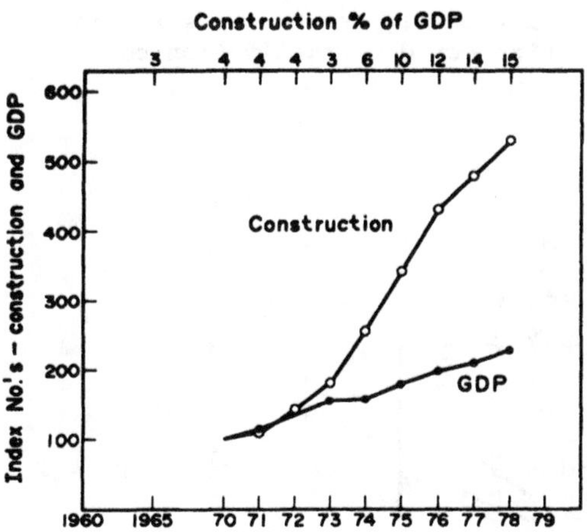

Figure 2.11: Nigeria

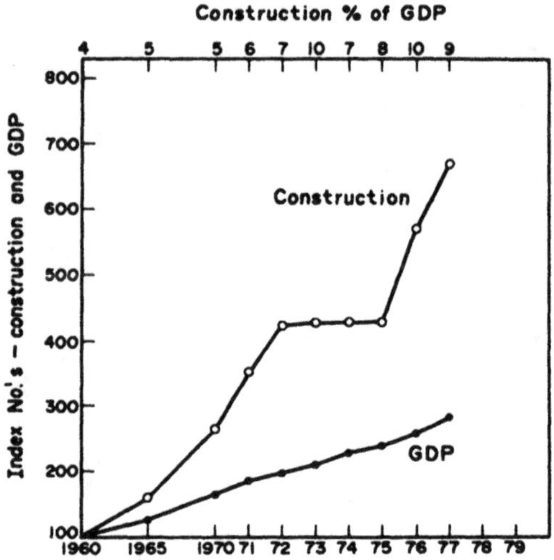

Figures 2.12 to 2.14: The Relationship between Construction Output and National Income in selected Centrally-Planned Economies

Figure 2.12: Yugoslavia

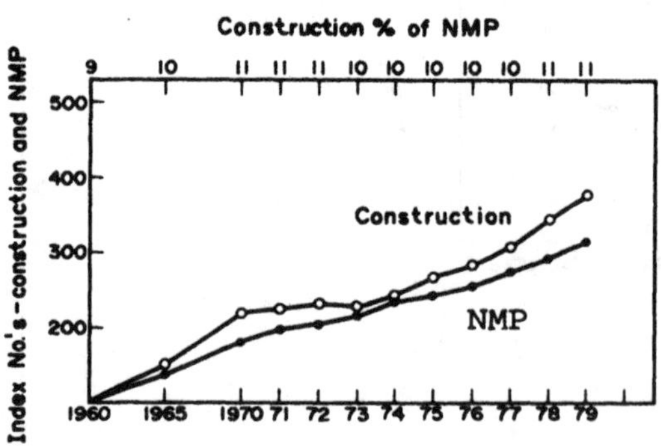

Figure 2.13: Romania

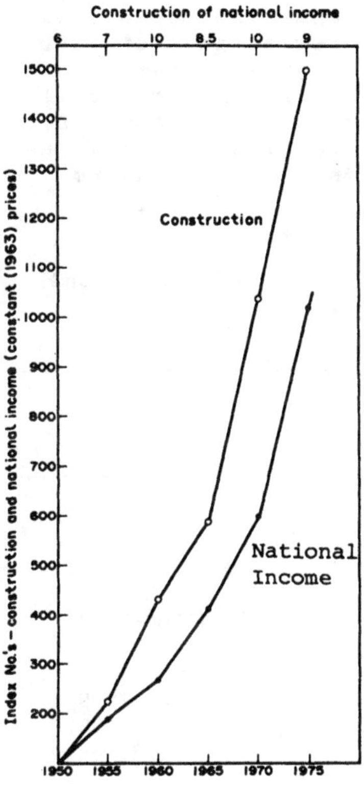

Figure 2.14: Cuba

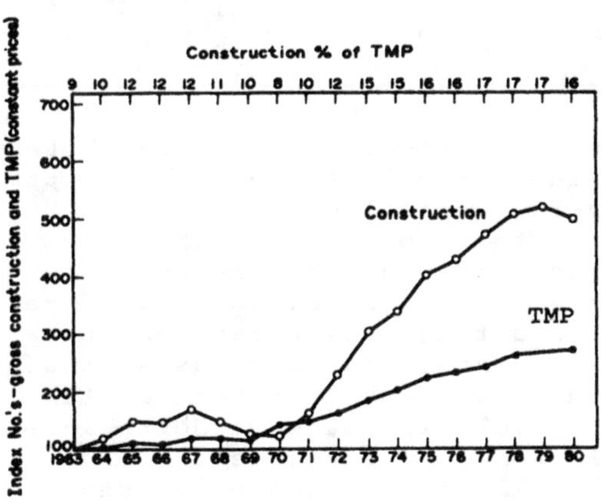

the countries selected for analysis, the relationship between the two variables is quite clear. During periods of expansion, when national income is growing, construction output does grow at an even faster rate - thus assuming an increasing percentage of GDP/NMP. And this appears to be true for centrally-planned economies as well as for market economies; for those without significant quantities of oil, as well as for oil-exporting states. Table 2.4 summarises the situation.

Table 2.4: Average Annual Growth Rates of Construction and GDP in Selected Countries, 1960-1979.

	Constr. %	GDP %	Notes
Group I			
South Korea	15.8	9.6	
Singapore	9.7	8.3	
Philippines	9.2	5.7	(1963-1979)
Morocco	11.3	4.9	(1960-1977)
Group II			
Mexico	7.9	6.3	
Equador	9.7	7.1	(1965-1979)
Saudi Arabia	15.0	11.1	(1963-1978)
Nigeria	21.1	7.7	(1970-1977 only)
Group III			
Yugoslavia	6.1	5.9	
Romania	11.3	9.7	(1950-1975)
Cuba	19.8	7.9	(1970-1978 only)

In all of the 11 countries selected, there has been significant and sustained growth of GDP over the past twenty years, with average annual growth rates ranging from 5 per cent to 11 per cent. In every case, however, construction output has grown at a faster rate, with annual averages ranging from 6 per cent to 15 per cent; and this growth rate has been sustained over 15 to 20 years. In many cases, the growth rate of construction output has been quite dramatic - with fifteen-fold increase in South Korea, a ten-fold increase in Romania, and a seven-fold increase in Singapore, all in a period of 20 years, and all in countries without oil. Over a shorter term, increases in individual countries have been even more spectacular - with a quadrupling of output in eight years in Cuba, a quintupling in eight years in Saudi Arabia, and a doubling in six years in Nigeria. In Mexico, Yugoslavia and Equador, construction output has quadrupled in a period of twenty years - less spectacular, but still impressive nonetheless.[10]

THE CASE FOR STRENGTHENING DOMESTIC CONSTRUCTION CAPACITY

What conclusions may be drawn from the above analysis? First, the close relationship between construction activity and economic growth can no longer be in dispute. Construction is a major component - arguably the major component of investment programmes. Therefore, during periods of accelerating economic growth, construction output grows at a faster rate than the economy as a whole. Inadequate construction capacity could act as a constraint on capital investment programmes. Investment and the rate of growth will be slowed down - and may eventually grind to a halt. Once construction has sufficient volume to raise the productive capacity of other sectors at a steady growth rate, its own growth could slow down - although over-expansion and subsequent decline have, in market economies, been more common.

Thus the expansion in the demand for construction products would seem to be most rapid during the early stages of development, in countries which are still at relatively low levels of income. This is also due to the fact that, in the course of national integration, industrialisation and urbanisation, basic infrastructure is still being put in place. It may also in part reflect that construction resources, in addition to satisfying a demand for investment in productive facilities, are also required for the satisfaction of one of the most basic human needs - the need for shelter; and in this respect there may be a huge backlog of suppressed demand to be accommodated. Thus, the expansion of construction output in middle-income countries would seem to be due to a rapid increase in both 'growth-initiating' and 'growth-dependent' construction.[11] The effects of the two together may cause some very spectacular rates of growth of construction output indeed - such as have in fact been observed in a number of countries during the past twenty years.

What then are the implications for countries where construction activity, far from growing over the past few decades, has actually stagnated - or even declined? Countries such as Tanzania, where construction output, at three per cent of GDP, is lower than it 'should be'? In fact, if OPEC/NIC countries are excluded, the figure for construction output as a percentage of GDP in the remaining developing countries appears remarkably stable - an average of 4.6 per cent in Asia and Latin America, and only 4.2 per cent in Africa. Nor should it be forgotten that these are percentages of very low levels of GDP - hence the absolute level of construction investment in these countries may be very low indeed, and a minute fraction of what it is in the developed world.[12] Without wishing to appear in any sense deterministic, or to jump to conclusions without due cause, it seems quite reasonable to assume that whenever economic growth does occur, or resume, in these countries in the future, there will necessarily be an immediate and rapid expansion in the demand for the products of the construction sector. Temporary upturns in economic activity, such as occurred in Kenya in 1967, and in Tanzania in 1964 and 1978, would certainly support this assumption.[13]

The immediate question raised by this conclusion is how the required expansion of construction activity may be brought about? Where are the additional resources to come from? They may of course be imported - either as individual items (of material, plant, manpower etc.), or as a part of a package offered by an international contracting organisation. There are two difficulties inherent in this course of action, however. First, resources of the kind required may not always be readily available; building materials that can be transported over long distances, or skilled manpower willing to work in remote up-country areas, are examples which immediately come to mind. Secondly, and most important, is the fact that even if resources are available, they have to be paid for, and paid for in foreign currency. While this may represent no problem to countries with substantial reserves of oil, or other highly marketable commodities, for the majority of developing countries today it is just inconceivable that construction resources (manpower, materials or machines), on the scale required for continuous economic growth, could be obtained through importation. For the current shortage of foreign exchange throughout the developing world, although obviously exacerbated by recent events in the world economy, is not just a short-term problem but rather a situation endemic to countries in the early stages of economic growth which have little prospect of expanding their exports or of increasing the inflow of capital (public or private) from abroad. Thus it seems that while it may be both necessary and feasible to import additional construction resources from time to time in order to cope with short-term fluctuations in demand, for the majority of developing countries the possibility of importing - and continuing to import over an extended period of time - the basic resources required for the expansion of the construction sector, does not really exist.

The only real alternative to the importation of construction resources lies in the development and expansion of domestic resources within developing countries themselves. In fact the vast majority of countries would seem to have no option but to attempt to create an indigenous construction capacity - based as far as possible upon the development of indigenous materials, manpower and technology - if economic growth in the long-term is to be sustained. Failure to do so must present the risk of failure to continue to grow in periods of reduced foreign-exchange earnings or international recession.

The benefits of the creation of a strong, viable domestic construction capacity in all countries - and especially in developing countries - are readily apparent. The existence of such a capacity would serve to reduce a country's dependence on imported materials and skills for the construction sector - and the 'leakage' to the economy that such importation represents - thus, economising on the use of scarce resources of foreign-exchange and obviating the development of foreign-exchange constraints on the execution of development programmes. At time of growth, these advantages would manifest themselves immediately. But even in the absence of economic growth, the development of local construction resources to serve local needs could provide a much-needed boost to employment and a means for redistributing income (especially to the rural areas) - as well as arguably laying the groundwork for the creation of a more integrated national economy.

How then is such a capacity to be created? The short answer is 'with difficulty'. Construction industries in many countries (particularly small countries in Africa, with which this study is most concerned) are currently at a very low level of development, and many countries rely to a very large extent upon the importation of resources for the execution of their construction programmes. In fact, foreign-exchange constraints on the implementation of development plans are already apparent - even at the present low levels of activity in the construction sector. An idea of the nature and scale of the problem is provided in Chapter three.

NOTES

1. See for example Graham Ive 'The Changing Interface between the Construction Industry and the Building Materials Industry in Britain: Hypothesis and Examples'. Paper presented to the Bartlett International Summer School, Bartlett School of Architecture and Planning, University College, London, 1982.

2. 'Force account' is the term used when a client himself engages in the construction process with his own directly-employed labour force.

3. For an interesting survey of the literature and summary of interpretations see Caroline Moser 'The Informal Sector or Petty Commodity Production: Autonomy or Dependence in Urban Development', Development Planning Unit Working Paper no. 3 (DPU, Bartlett School of Architecture and Planning, University College London, 1978).

4. This is the sense in which the term 'informal sector' is generally understood when used in reference to construction.

5. Including two recent and important documents in this field: (1) G.A. Edmonds and D.W.J. Miles, Foundations for Change: Aspects of the Construction Industry in Developing Countries. (Intermediate Technology Publications, 1984) and (2) The World Bank, The Construction Industry: Issues and Strategies in Developing Countries (World Bank, Washington, 1984).

6. Value-added by construction to GDP is the measure adopted according to the 'System of National Accounts' used in market economies; the equivalent under the 'System of Material Product Balances' used by the majority of centrally-planned economies, is the contribution of construction output to Net Material Product, or NMP. The measures are not strictly comparable.

7. Such methods include simply dividing population growth by average family size to arrive at a figure for additional number of households; it is then assumed that additional households are in fact accommodated. Also construction is assumed to

equal differences in the housing stock in two census years, which ignores replacement.

8. A similar analysis was conducted by Turin and the University College Environmental Research Group (UCERG) in the late 1960s and published by a number of sources; see, for example, UNIDO, 'Construction Industry', Monograph No. 2, New York, ID/40/2, 1969. A similar analysis was conducted by Strassmann at about the same time; see Strassmann, W.P. 'The Construction Sector in Economic Development, Scottish Journal of Political Economy 17, 1970.

9. Construction output is measured 'net' (i.e. value-added) except in the case of Cuba, where it is measured as gross output. Income is represented by GDP in the market economies, and NMP in the centrally-planned economies - both net measures. The exception again is Cuba, where income is represented by TMP (Total Material Product) which is a gross output measure including only the productive sectors of the economy, i.e. industry, mining, agriculture, fishing and construction; this difference in the method of measurement is immaterial for present purposes, except that it means construction's share of total income will be exaggerated.

10. By way of comparison, it is interesting to note that in Europe after the Second World War the output of the construction industry only tripled in a period of 20 years; yet this created an enormous strain on the construction industries of individual countries, and necessitated strong action on the part of governments to secure a structural and technological transformation; see United Nations, Economic Commission for Europe (UN/ECE), Human Settlements in Europe: Post-War Trends and Policies, New York, ECE/HBP/18, 1976.

11. The distinction is drawn by Drewer; see Drewer, S. 'Construction and Development: a New Perspective', Habitat International 5(3/4), 1980.

12. Edmonds and Miles point out that the two extremes for investment in construction per head of population around 1979 were Norway: 2070 dollars per-capita and Ethiopia: 6 dollars per capita; see Edmonds and Miles, Foundations for Change, page 10.

13. Others might go further and argue that construction output must expand quickly in these countries, irrespective of whether or not there is economic growth. This is necessary, so the argument goes, in order to improve upon the present low standards of shelter, and to cater for the additional

housing needs arising from rapid population growth and rural to urban migration. Unfortunately such advocates of rapid expansion of output from the construction sector fail to distinguish between need and effective demand for housing; thus, while the need for additional investment in housing is obvious, the means of financing it is not. The result of sudden expansion in the demand for housing, in the absence of general expansion in the economy as a whole, is generally rapid inflation, accompanied by the development of foreign-exchange constraints. Such was the experience of Colombia; see L. Parsons-Fox. *Building Construction as an Engine of Economic Growth: An Evaluation* (University of North Carolina, 1976).

Chapter Three

UNDER-DEVELOPED RESOURCES

Following the attainment of political independence in the 1950s and 1960s, many countries in Africa and Asia launched ambitious development plans, involving high levels of investment, much of it in basic infrastructure. This required a rapid expansion (in both qualitative and quantitative terms) of activity in the construction sector - which in many countries had been inactive for a number of years due to the uncertainties surrounding independence. It was not long before weaknesses in the domestic construction industry became apparent. In one country after another, 'inadequate capacity in the construction sector' was singled out as the major cause of the failure to implement development projects and to meet the targets set out in development plans.[1]

CONSTRUCTION CAPACITY IN KENYA, 1967

Kenya was no exception to this pattern. The first five year development plan was launched in 1965. By 1967 there was considerable concern among various ministries and government departments at the low level of construction activity since the beginning of the five-year plan period. This concern was not without foundation. As independence approached, with its attendant uncertainties, there was a slump in the private building sector. Consequently construction activity declined from 39.7 per cent of GFCF in 1956 to only 17.6 per cent in 1963. While the level of investment in the economy (GFCF) started to increase in 1964, and by 1966 had reached an all-time high, only a small part of this investment was in construction. In 1966, construction investment accounted for only 15.5 per cent of GFCF - its lowest ever recorded level. In addition to the disappointingly low levels of construction activity, between 1965 and 1967 there was a sharp rise in construction prices, causing particular concern to public bodies operating on fixed annual budgets.[2] These two factors together (the inadequacy of construction activity and the sharp rise in prices) - appeared to many in the Kenya government at the time to be a clear indication of the effective demand for construction outstripping the supply - or the development of a 'constraint' on the supply side of the industry. This fear found expression in the 1967 Economic Survey, which pointed out the shortfall in actual as against planned expenditures and attributed this 'particularly to construction delays in planned capital works'.[3] The Survey in fact went further than this and cited the inability of the building industry to gear itself to the much higher level of construction activity required by Government for the implementation of its development plans as one of the major causes of this shortfall.

A shortage of actual as against planned development expenditure on construction can of course be due to a number of causes other than inadequate capacity in the construction sector. It may equally, and perhaps more probably, be due to delays and bottlenecks arising in the financing and planning of development projects, i.e. delays arising within the government machinery, on the demand side of the industry. There was little doubt that these impediments were operating in Kenya in 1967, as in many other newly-independent countries with little experience of the planning process. But nonetheless, inadequate construction capacity, giving rise to constraints on the supply side of the industry, could not be ruled out as a further factor affecting the level of construction activity. Supply constraints may in fact manifest themselves in a number of ways. First, in the *physical* sense of an actual failure to implement projects, perhaps due to the inability of the client to engage contractors (or designers) willing to do the work; or if designs are completed and contractors are engaged, it may be due to subsequent delays in the execution of the work (and hence a constraint on the volume of work completed in a given time) arising from the failure on the part of contractors to obtain vital inputs of materials, manpower or machines. Secondly, even if there is no physical constraint on implementation, there may be a constraint in the *financial* sense - as rising prices (themselves indicative of the development of shortages in the market for one or more vital inputs) serve to limit the volume of work that can be carried out with fixed financial resources. In Kenya in 1967, prices were rising rapidly, despite the fact that output was still at a very low level. It therefore seemed quite likely that delays and rising prices were indicative of the fact that supply constraints had already developed in the construction sector. And if this was the case, then it was clearly a factor that would assume greater significance, with expanded volumes of work, in the future. A detailed investigation was carried out into the conditions of supply in the Kenyan construction industry, the results of which will be briefly outlined, in order that it may serve as a basis for comparison with subsequent studies elsewhere.[4]

Firstly, evidence of constraint in the physical sense of a failure on the part of clients to engage contractors or designers to implement construction projects proved difficult to obtain in Kenya in 1967. There was clearly no shortage of design capacity, with many public-sector clients of the construction industry having their own well-staffed design offices and a large number of private professional design offices in Nairobi and Mombasa (as well as in some of the smaller towns) only too anxious to expand their activities. There also seemed to be no shortage of contractors willing and able to tender for medium or large, public or private sector, contracts. In fact, analysis from clients' records of a total of 248 such contracts awarded during the years 1965, 1966 and 1967, revealed that in no instance did the number of tenders received for any one contract fall below five; there was no evidence of any increase in the number of firms invited to tender who failed to do so; and no significant rise in the price variation on tenders submitted.[5] Physical constraint in the tender market did not seem to be apparent.

This conclusion was substantiated by the evidence presented by contractors themselves. There were in fact a considerable number of contracting firms operating in Kenya in 1967. Eleven of these were large European-owned firms, two of them public limited companies of an 'international' kind. There were 33 large Asian-owned firms, with a certain minimum of capital invested in fixed assets and a core of permanent skilled staff; 76 small Asian firms of a 'one-man' kind; and just under 200 firms owned by Africans - although many of these existed in name only, and only about 12 of them had proven capacity on a par with the smallest of the Asian companies.[6] Interviews with a large cross-section of these contracting firms revealed that each group had certain distinguishing characteristics and was either obliged or chose to operate within a clearly-defined field. Thus there was not really one tender market but several. On the other hand, there was found to be a high degree of complementarity between firms and a fair degree of mobility in terms of the area of operation and the size of the projects upon which they would work. So that although the larger firms preferred to work on larger projects in Nairobi, there were plenty of smaller firms scattered throughout the country who were happy to work on small jobs in the more remote areas. The evidence of contractors themselves in fact confirmed that there was no shortage of companies active in the market, no difficulty in persuading them to tender and subsequently carry out contracts and a high level of competition still existing among them. Thus, inadequate capacity in the construction industry, in terms of contractors, could not be held responsible for the relatively low level of construction activity in Kenya during 1965 to 1967.

Considerable disquiet was expressed, however, by both clients and contractors regarding the availability and price of building materials. In addition, there were complaints on the part of clients about a fall in the standards of quality of work completed; and there also seemed to be an almost universal reluctance among contractors to undertake any kind of high quality building work involving complicated finishes or structures. It appeared likely that these factors were not unconnected, and that an explanation might be found in the markets for the various factors of production - particularly skilled labour and materials.

The Labour Market

As a factor of production 'labour' is quite clearly not a homogeneous commodity. The general difficulty of division and definition within the labour market is complicated in the construction industry by the fact that formal training and qualifications are often less important than experience 'on-the-job' and therefore provide unreliable guides to the actual value of an employee. Thus a man with no formal education may be undertaking a very responsible job and commanding a far higher salary than a recent trade school graduate with a 'Grade I' trade test.[7]

A further difficulty arises in the field of job-content. What a man actually does on the construction site, particularly in terms of organisation, supervision and the general exercise of responsibility, may be quite different from that which his formal position or title implies; a 'joiner' may in fact be involved in general supervision, while a 'foreman' may be nothing more than a man in charge of one simple operation. The casual nature of employment in the industry adds further to the difficulties. Thus, in dividing the construction site labour force into three categories of (1) supervisors, (2) artisans or craftsmen and (3) semi-skilled and unskilled labour, it must be borne in mind that the three categories are not clear-cut; substitution is particularly important between categories 1 and 2 and there exists a very wide range of ability within each.

Prior to independence, the construction industry in Kenya was almost exclusively the preserve of non-citizens, particularly those of Asian origin - descendents of the Indians originally brought over to East Africa by the British, for construction of the railways. And both Asian and European-owned firms filled their middle and high level posts with skilled and experienced artisans and supervisors from the Asian community. An indeterminate number of Africans did receive, even before independence, a minimum of formal training in the more basic craft skills of masonry, carpentry or painting - either from the trade schools, or from the missions. Some of these found employment in the public sector and some were taken on by European firms, mostly as lower grade craftsmen. Few of the Asian firms, however, which comprised the backbone of the industry, employed Africans in any capacity above that of unskilled, casual labour. And there were no African contractors, as described above. Thus many African graduates of the trade schools found it impossible to gain employment in the industry. A number of them were eventually absorbed into activities unrelated to their training.

At the end of the 1950s a slump in construction activity, together with a good deal of uncertainty engendered by the imminent approach of political independence and uncertain status of the Asian community, led to a large-scale 'exodus' of Asians from all of the East African countries. It would appear to have been particularly severe among the supervisory and artisan grade of building labour - skills for which there are good employment opportunities in many parts of the world. This exodus of skilled construction labour was accompanied, at least since independence, by a conscious attempt on the part of the Kenyan Government to encourage the employment and upgrading of Africans in the industry. The attempt seemed, however, to have found only limited response. Although reactions in the industry varied, in general the casual nature of employment and the very real and imminent danger of losing trained employees to other firms (other industries or other countries) militated against the recruitment of apprentices or the upgrading of African labour through the provision of training 'on-the-job'. Thus by 1967 there were a fair number of Africans with the more basic skills and some experience of work in trades such as carpentry, painting or masonry; but there were very few with the higher types of artisan skills such as joinery and practically no Africans employed in any kind of supervisory capacity - or even in the process of being trained for supervision. Thus, with the gradual run-down of the skilled Asian labour force, in the absence of any systematic training or upgrading programme for Africans, and against a background of rising construction activity, there existed in Kenya in 1967 a severe shortage of artisans and supervisors.

The effects of this severe shortage of skilled labour are not difficult to envisage. First, it would seem to offer an adequate explanation for the reluctance on the part of contractors to undertake any kind of high quality building work, as it is in these kinds of projects that the requirements for both high artisan skills and expert supervision are the most demanding. Physical constraint in this section of the market, if not already apparent, seemed imminent. Secondly, with contractors forced to compete for the small supply of Asian and more experienced African labour available, wages were forced up well above the official minimum for the various grades of craftsmen. Apart from the obvious implication of higher costs to the contractor, and hence higher tender prices, a further significant effect was that contractors who were unable or unwilling to pay the high wages required to attract competent supervisory staff, did without - with a consequent 'dilution' of supervision, lower productivity of labour and falling standards of work. Thus both higher prices and a fall in the quality of work could be traced back to the situation in the labour market. In the absence of significant corrective measures (such as a programme for the importation of supervisory skills or a crash training programme) the rise in the price and fall in quality and efficiency of work could be expected, in the face of further expansion of activity in the construction sector, to spread and intensify.

The Materials Market

The situation regarding the supply of building materials and components to the construction industry was as serious as the situation in the labour market. The general practice in most countries is for materials and supplies to be 'bought-in' by a contractor from an independent supplier. This frees the contractor from a great deal of responsibility, and also from the obligation to tie up his capital in fixed assets, thereby giving him much greater flexibility for manoeuvre in the tender market. In Kenya these purchased materials may be divided for purposes of analysis into three broad categories. First, there are a number of products used in construction which have to be imported from outside the country, or the region;[8] these include steel products (rods, bars and tubes), sanitary fittings, glass, tiles and other types of high value or special components. Secondly, there are a number of products manufactured in factories in Kenya or other countries of the East African region, such as cement, asbestos, window frames, tiles etc. And thirdly, there are a number of unprocessed or semi-processed products of a heavy, bulky nature - unfinished timber and quarry products such as sand, stone and aggregates; these are characterised by the fact that they are produced locally, for local markets, where they frequently enjoy a high degree of natural protection (owing to the high cost of transport) and therefore are peculiarly prone to monopoly conditions in production and marketing.

Serious problems affecting the supply of the first two of these groups of products were found to lie in the field of transport and distribution. With the slump in construction and the uncertainty regarding the future operations of non-citizens in Kenya, builders merchants (the vast majority of whom were of the Asian community) had been running down their stocks. After independence the general feeling of uncertainty was increased by a number of political decisions - such as those relating to the issue, or re-issue, of trade licences and the reservation of certain products to African distributors - so that the wholesale and distribution network in some parts of the country became quite seriously disrupted, with consequent delays of up to six months for the delivery of certain items. This situation of course imposed additional financial and organisational strains upon the contractor, who was obliged to plan ahead, and place orders well in advance of delivery dates.

In addition to problems in the field of distribution, there were a number of difficulties in the production of building materials in East Africa in 1967. Long delays were recorded (up to nine months) in the delivery of asbestos sheets from the factory in Tororo, Uganda - which has a monopoly of the Kenyan market for asbestos products, but inadequate capacity to cope with the demand. Similarly, there was a five-month delay in the receipt of steel windows from two factories in Kenya, one in Nairobi and one in Mombasa. And considerable concern was also expressed over the inadequacy of the supply of joinery products produced in small workshops largely owned by Asian artisans. By far the most serious problem in the supply of building materials, however, was found to lie in the production and marketing of quarry products - rough, unprocessed, bulky materials such as sand, aggregates and stone. Serious difficulties were noted in the availability of these products throughout the country, with shortages especially severe in the smaller towns. In addition, prices were found to have increased virtually overnight by anything up to 200 per cent, which was well above the general level of inflation and far in excess of any increase in costs. There was a widespread belief that they would rise again in line with any further increase in demand. Detailed investigation of the quarrying industry revealed it to be almost exclusively in the hands of the Asian community. Quarries were severely under-capitalised, with a level of investment more appropriate for short-term profits than long-term efficiency; there was no attempt at rational planning or organisation of production, so that supplies were inadequate in terms of both quantity and quality; and quarry-owners, enjoying a position of monopoly in many local markets, were perfectly able and willing to use their power to determine both output and price in their own interests. Where there were more than one or two owners, producers' 'rings', or unofficial cartels, were found to be operating to similar effect.[9] Yet despite these serious inadequacies in the supply of some of the most basic products of construction, and the fact that there was clearly no incentive for producers to behave any differently in the future, very few contractors seemed willing to enter into the materials supply industries and start producing quarry products for their own use ... a situation which may well have had more to do with the uncertainties associated with the system of competitive tendering and consequent reluctance to invest in fixed capital assets than with the fact that the majority of contractors and quarry-owners were non-citizens of the country in which they were operating.[10]

Thus analysis of the conditions of supply in the Kenyan construction industry in 1967 revealed no shortage of contractors. Many of them were actively looking for work and competition in the tender market was, by all accounts, still relatively keen. There were serious shortages, however, in the factor markets - particularly in the supply of skilled and experienced labour, and a number of the more basic materials; and there was a lack of forward planning in the wholesale and distribution industries. These problems were themselves the direct cause of rising prices and increased contractor costs. They were also found to be responsible for the marked fall in the quality of work, and reduction in efficiency throughout the industry.[11]

Despite these difficulties, there appeared to be no constraint in the strict physical sense to the implementation of construction projects in Kenya. But prices were rising and financial constraints had begun to appear. Whether or not these were the result of temporary 'hiccups' in supply, as the construction industry geared itself up for a higher level of activity than it had been used to in the past would depend upon the extent to which high prices in the factor markets might serve to stimulate the mobilisation of additional resources of labour and materials. In view of the degree of imperfection in the market for building materials and the long-run nature of any solution to the training problem, this possibility appeared unlikely. The supply curve of the construction industry, if not vertical, must be steeply upward-sloping ... at least in the short and medium term. The chances of cost reduction seemed to be slim.[12]

Chapter Three

THE CONSTRUCTION INDUSTRY IN TANZANIA, 1968-1985

This gloomy prognosis for the construction industry in Kenya in 1967 is significant. For it should be noted that Kenya was an especially favoured country within East Africa. Not only did it experience a high degree of settlement (by both Europeans and Asians) during colonial times, but it was also deliberately promoted by the colonial authorities as the industrial and commercial centre of the region. As a result it had at independence a reasonable transport and distribution network, a fair industrial base and a relatively well-developed construction sector - albeit once owned and operated by non-citizens. Of even greater significance, independent Kenya inherited a buoyant export sector and consequently suffered no immediate and crippling shortage of foreign-exchange - so that materials, equipment and all levels of manpower required for the construction sector could, if necessary, be imported fairly freely into the country from abroad. Despite these advantages, the situation in the construction sector still gave cause for concern.

In Tanzania there was even more reason for alarm. At independence in 1961 the level of development of African labour was lower even than in Kenya - with no Africans employed in the construction sector above the level of 'general foreman'. The transportation and distribution network was also substantially less developed than in Kenya. And there were very few construction materials produced domestically and virtually no quarries in operation at all outside of the major towns. Contractors were obliged to attempt to import their material requirements from abroad, or where this was quite impossible, to simply produce their own.

Even more serious was the situation in the contracting market. It is a characteristic perhaps peculiar to Tanzania that, even some ten years after independence, there were still no African contractors. Although there had been a number of European and Asian firms, very few of these were still around following the pre- and post-independence 'slump' which lasted from 1960 to 1963. Hence, the recovery in the level of investment and construction, which began in 1964 and continued until 1973, was accompanied by steadily rising prices, complaints of shortages in the tender market and an inability on the part of some clients to find a contractor at *any* price - indicating the development of physical constraint. Was the local construction industry unable to cope?

Detailed investigation of the contracting, or tender, market undertaken in 1968 showed that these fears were in fact justified.[13] As in Kenya, there was not one tender market but several, the market being stratified both functionally (according to the size of the contract and the degree of complexity of the structure) and geographically. The following subdivisions were identified: (1) a market for small projects (under £20,000 in value) involving buildings of one, two or three storeys, but of a relatively simple nature; (2) a market for complex buildings - including high-rise perhaps with complex services, requiring a high standard of construction and/or above £20,000 in value; (3) a market for civil-engineering projects of all kinds; and (4) a 'catch-all' of specialist structures, mostly commercial buildings. These functional divisions were overlain by regional divisions - with the market for small buildings being essentially local in character, those for civil-engineering and specialist structures being national in scope and the market for complex building falling somewhere between the two extremes. Each market was the preserve of a separate but not exclusive, group of firms. Interviews were conducted with a large sample of firms operating in each of these market sub-divisions and the following picture emerged.

First, the market for simple buildings (or more precisely 'markets', there being a more or less separate market for each town) was found to be served by small Asian-owned firms. With low barriers to entry into this industry and the minimum requirement of fixed assets for operation in the small building market, the exact number of firms in this category could not be determined with any degree of accuracy. In fact it seemed to fluctuate widely in line with the opportunities in the building market and those available elsewhere. Thus, 44 potential builders were identified in Dar-Es-Salaam but only about half of these were actually active in the tender market at the time and dependent entirely upon the award of building contracts for their livelihood. According to the contractors themselves, tendering in this market was fairly keen *only* until contractors have reached approximately 60 per cent of their capacity, or 'break-even point' - after which they submitted much higher-priced tenders to compensate for what they thought had been lost on the earlier low bids. This means in essence that the market 'goes soft' long before capacity with present resources is reached; so that above a certain level of activity prices will tend to rise quite independently of costs. Thus, although with a number of firms tendering there may have been some semblance of competition in this particular market, or section of the market, the volume of work in Dar-Es-Salaam from 1964 onwards was substantial - and certainly sufficient to indicate that contractors must have been earning significant returns for several years. The hostile reaction of these small firms to the occasional entry of aggressive new companies into their market would seem to substantiate the point.

There were far fewer firms operating in the market for large and/or complex building structures in Tanzania. None of these was African - although there was one 'parastatal' firm, partly owned by the Tanzanian government.[14] Of the total of 12 privately-owned firms in this group, three were large 'international' firms run by Asians and expatriates; a further nine were 'family' firms owned and operated by local, non-citizen Asians. Only one half of these firms had, however, actually carried out a building contract greater than £250,000 in value - which indicates that the competition for really large projects was none too keen. In fact, it was found that the top five companies were responsible for 75 per cent of the work done in this category. With such a limited number of firms, and in the face of a consistently high level of demand throughout the latter part of the 1960s, the number of firms who were actively looking for work at any one time was very small - and profit margins comensurably high. This particular market must be 'soft' for much of the time.

If profit margins were high in large building works, in civil-engineering they were even higher. The very large works in this field were undertaken almost exclusively by international firms based mostly outside of Tanzania. Competition was all but absent; but when it threatened, organisations seemed to get together and collude. Consequently, prices on particular projects were as much as 100 per cent above the estimates; profits were enormous - as were the foreign-exchange costs of such projects.[15] For smaller jobs in this category, competition from smaller, local firms was conceivable but this should not be exaggerated; in 1968 only four such firms were operating in Dar-Es-Salaam, and they also undertook building work. Outside the capital, such small firms scarcely exist.

Finally, there is the 'special structures' section of the market, supplied by only three firms -

one producing reinforced concrete frame structures, one erecting imported steel structures, and the third producing structures from steel sections which were manufactured locally. These three firms, all European-owned, had chosen this section of the market simply because there was virtually no competition; in fact the firms had quite successfully insulated themselves from whatever competition there might have been (in the general building market for commercial structures) through product differentiation and a very successful marketing operation. Prices therefore reflected this monopolistic situation.

Thus the conclusion that emerged from the study of the contracting market in Tanzania in 1968 was that the effects of competition were felt only in a very few, isolated areas of the market. The number of firms interested in tendering for any particular contract at any particular time depended upon the size of the contract and the degree of complexity of the structure. It also depended upon the geographical location of the project and the current level of commitment of the contractors operating in that section of the market, in that particular location. In general, small contracts interested only small, local firms; very large and complex jobs interested only a few national contractors; maximum interest could therefore be expected for a substantial contract made up of simple structures. In fact the best performance was registered in the market for the building of warehouses and in contracts for the erection of a large number of simple repetitive structures on one site. With this exception, all other areas of the market were characterised by a serious lack of competition, high contract prices and large profits.

This conclusion was supported some ten years later when the Tanzanian Government, through its Ministry of Works, initiated a further study of the construction sector. The problems were by then pretty well-known; the objective of the study was therefore to 'identify factors contributing to present problems in construction and recommend suitable steps to correct them'.[16] A team of experts was recruited, from the Building Research Unit and from abroad, for the purpose. The report concluded (as had the earlier study) that the amount of competition in the tender market varied according to the size of contract and the geographical location. There was competition among Asian contractors for small jobs in Dar-Es-Salaam but for all larger contracts there were only a handful of contractors (European and Asian) with the required capacity and they were able to dominate the market and command high prices. In addition, small contracts in rural areas were seldom sought by the private contracting industry - and ministries were sometimes unable to persuade any contractor to even consider submitting a tender. As a result, at least in part, of this constant imbalance between requirements and capacities, prices rose at anything from 10 per cent to 40 per cent per annum, depending on the type of construction; and this was in spite of the fact that construction activity had been declining from the peak reached in 1973. With wide profit margins there was little incentive for contractors to attempt to improve upon the generally low level of efficiency prevalent in the construction industry.[17]

Underlying the high profits and poor performance of contractors, the report also revealed a serious shortage of skilled manpower, particularly supervisory staff, throughout the construction industry. The majority of construction labour (even those with some craft skills) was still recruited on a casual daily basis, and frequently paid less than the minimum legal rates. Very few contractors were willing to recruit and train craft apprentices; there was no course in supervision for construction foremen; no 'acclimatisation' training for expatriate professionals or Tanzanian graduates returning from abroad; and no university courses, inside Tanzania, in either construction or design. The consequent lack of skilled craftsmen, foremen, supervisors, professionals, and middle and senior level management in construction firms had detrimental effects upon the level of craftsmanship and efficiency. And even more serious than the current situation was the apparent trend towards deterioration - as experienced men left the industry for various reasons, to be replaced by untrained and inexperienced personnel.[18] Against this background of inadequate levels of training and up-grading within the construction industry it was not surprising to find that in Tanzania (even in the later 1970s) there were still no significant African contracting firms.

As well as these serious problems in the labour market, contractors were also facing in the later 1970s a series of bottlenecks and shortages in the supply of building materials, equipment and spare parts. There were frequent and sustained shortages of cement, causing increased costs and delays to a number of projects. There was no ready-mix concrete plant in Tanzania, despite clear indications of sufficient demand for one to be established in Dar-Es-Salaam, and possibly also in Dodoma. The quarrying industry was seriously run-down, and urgently in need of reorganisation and expansion; and there was also much room for improvement in the quality of aggregates produced and hence in the quality of concrete products such as blocks, pipes and kerbs. Burnt lime was expensive, and production capacity in need of expansion. Facilities for the production of burnt clay bricks (the demand for which had increased owing to shortages of cement) needed to be examined, and production improved. There were frequent shortages of nails, as a result of worn-down machinery, little access to spare parts and difficulties with the importation of raw materials. And there were serious problems in the availability of steel and steel products which, along with bitumen, hardware, sanitaryware and electrical equipment, were imported from abroad.[19] In short, there were numerous serious shortages of materials components and spare parts for the construction industry which, in the 1970s, were delaying the progress of construction projects and hampering the implementation of development plans. Rationalisation and massive investment in the materials industry was clearly required.[20]

Since that time, the situation in the building materials and supply industries in Tanzania has deteriorated further, following a sudden drain in foreign-exchange reserves in 1979, and the subsequent developmentof chronic foreign-exchange problems.[21] By 1980, no imported building materials were available at all, except in the 'black market' at ridiculous prices. In addition, there were acute shortages of raw materials and machinery spare parts for the local production of manufactured, or semi-processed, materials - causing many products to be simply unobtainable due to the non-functioning of the factories, or subject to long delays in delivery due to less than capacity working.[22] Finally, there was also an acute shortage of spare parts for construction equipment, plant and transport, including a particularly severe and widespread shortage of tyres.

The immediate result of these shortages of materials, raw materials and spare parts are perhaps predictable: (1) delays in the completion of projects, aggravated by a further fall in the productivity of labour as materials are consumed at the slowest possible rate to ensure work for tomorrow; (2) a thriving black market for materials, with unofficial prices two or three times the official rate; and (3) a general feeling of extreme frustration on the part of contractors, as they are forced to spend much of their time searching for materials which, all too often, are simply not there. As a result of all of these factors, there have been further unprecedented increases in tender prices - representing both increased costs to the contractor and inflated profits, as fewer and fewer firms consider the frustrations of working in Tanzania to be worthwhile.[23] With a level of inflation in the construction sector estimated at 50 per cent per annum by late 1983 and with many projects grinding to a halt (either through lack of essential inputs or lack of funds) the construction industry in Tanzania in the mid 1980s is clearly suffering from both physical and financial constraints.[24]

CONSTRUCTION IN OTHER COUNTRIES : GHANA, SRI-LANKA, NIGERIA

The situation in the construction sector in Tanzania, although more serious than in Kenya, is by no means unique. Similar conditions have been noted in Ghana where as early as 1965 and again in 1974 the failure to implement development projects was attributed, by government, to inadequate capacity in the construction industry.[25] Investigation showed the problems facing the construction industry to be essentially similar to those identified in Kenya and Tanzania, i.e. (1) an unhealthy reliance upon imported materials, which may amount to up to 60 per cent of the total; (2) problems in the availability of locally-produced materials, including frequent shortages of cement, and inadequate capacity in the quarrying industry; and (3) serious shortages of skilled labour, due both to the absence of training programmes and to a failure to provide adequate rewards so as to prevent the loss of manpower, once trained, to other countries, industries or firms. As a result of all of these factors, costs were high and productivity low. By the late 1970s, high and rising prices and a worsening foreign-exchange situation seem to have caused the worst fears of government to come true - inadequate capacity in the construction sector was acting as a constraint, in both the physical and financial sense, upon the implementation of development plans.

Similarly, in Sri-Lanka the setting of ambitious output targets for the construction sector in 1977 was not accompanied by any serious concern or analysis of the inputs and resources required to achieve a significantly expanded volume of activity in the domestic construction industry. Consequently, imports of materials, raw materials, manpower and equipment rose rapidly and foreign-exchange costs were pushed up to between 50 per cent and 80 per cent of total costs. Eventually Sri-Lanka became dependent upon foreign contractors for as much as two-thirds of the total volume of work. But not all of the foreign-exchange costs were covered by foreign aid. With construction costs in general rising from between 40 per cent to 60 per cent per annum, there emerged after 1980 both foreign and domestic monetary constraints. The development programme had to be seriously curtailed.[26]

Finally, inadequacy in the supply of domestic construction resources is not a problem which is confined to countries saddled with large foreign debts and operating under conditions of severe foreign-exchange constraint. Even in Nigeria, where construction activity increased steadily from 3.5 per cent of GDP in 1959 to 7.7 per cent in 1973, where there were no shortages of foreign-exchange prior to the OPEC price-cuts and where a strong indigenous entrepreneurial tradition exists, the capacity of the domestic construction industry has, on a number of occasions, been the subject of concern. Thus in the early 1970s, in the face of an enormous expansion of capital spending, rising prices and delays in the implementation of development projects seemed to indicate that inadequate construction capacity may be operating as a bottleneck to further expansion of the economy.[27] Singled out for particular attention were the problems of low levels of training in the construction industry; poor organisation of the industry, with a large number of very small and inefficient firms; a lack of planning at all levels; poor site organisation and low labour productivity; and inadequate capacity and inefficiency in the building materials industries. In addition, there was considerable dissatisfaction expressed over the operation of the tender market and particularly over the fact that civil-engineering projects seemed to be almost a monopoly of the large foreign companies. There was also a noted lack of 'economic rationality' in design. Expansion and rationalisation of design, construction and the production of building materials was therefore called for, i.e. the rationalisation of the whole building process.

Chapter Three

SUMMARY AND CONCLUSIONS: PROBLEMS IN THE DEVELOPMENT OF THE CONSTRUCTION SECTOR

In conclusion, it must be said that the construction industry in developing countries today - with some notable exceptions - does not appear to be fulfilling its full potential role in economic growth and development. The actual performance of the construc tion sector in any particular country may in fact be evaluated against a number of indicators. These include: (1) the extent to which the construction projects in a country's development plan are actually implemented to time; (2) the percentage of imports in the total construction output; (3) the degree of development of local skills, and of local participation in contracting; (4) the extent of development of the local building materials industries; (5) the overall efficiency/productivity of the construction sector and the extent to which construction plans are implemented within the cost limits set. By any, or all, of these indicators, the vast majority of the (very large) number of developing countries for which information is now available fare very badly; the least developed countries among them fare worst of all.[28] The situation may be briefly summarised as follows.

First, in some countries there may be an actual inability to execute (or long delays in the completion of) a number of construction projects. This may be due to a variety of factors, such as inadequate capacity or inefficiency in the design and planning of projects; difficulty in obtaining tenders for small projects in which international contractors are not interested, or for projects which are too large for local contractors to handle; or difficulty in obtaining materials, skilled labour or other vital inputs. Whatever the cause, delays of this kind are common, and represent a physical constraint on development.

Secondly, in a large number of countries, the import-content of construction activity is high. According to one estimate up to 60 per cent of the value of all materials, may be imported - as well as a significant percentage of professional, managerial, supervisory and even craft skills.[29] In addition, most of the profits of the foreign-based construction or design firms, as well as the wages and salaries of foreign personnel, may be remitted out of the country. Thus, construction activity may impose a severe strain on the balance of payments - which may already be in a critical state due to deterioration in the terms of trade. In many countries therefore there is a foreign-exchange constraint on construction activity and the implementation of development plans.

The construction industry as a whole requires a higher percentage of skilled labour than does manufacturing. Within the construction sector, building requires a higher skill level than civil-engineering and repairs and maintenance the highest level of all. Also, highly-developed management and supervisory skills are crucial for the efficient execution of construction projects. Most developing countries have a severe shortage of all kinds of skilled labour for the construction industry and a large percentage of these skills have therefore to be imported. Moreover, apprenticeships and vocational training schemes appear to be grossly inadequate, in both quantitative and qualitative terms.[30] There may therefore be in many countries a skilled labour constraint on the expansion of construction activity.

In view of the situation in the labour market, it follows there is also in many countries a lack of development of the local contracting industry. The degree of local participation in contracting varies but it is common to find that, if there are some national contractors they operate only on the smallest projects, such as single houses - and this is the case even in countries where there exists a strong entrepreneurial tradition. It should be noted that there are enormous difficulties and risks inherent in the contracting business and a very wide variety of skills is required, particularly the skills which in developing countries are in short supply. Some kind of technical training and some supervisory or organisation experience are perhaps the basic minimum of skills that are needed; in addition, a successful contractor must be able to read and interpret drawings, to understand the complications of tendering and contractual procedures and to be able to take care of insurances, bonds and other legal necessities. He must also be in a position to secure sufficient working capital and/or materials credit to finance his projects, even when payment by the client (as so often happens) is delayed.[31]

Construction materials industries in developing countries are also generally undeveloped, or inadequate to meet demands. A number of countries now have some installed capacity for cement production and some in fact have a surplus for export. But there still appear to be frequent and severe bottlenecks in the supply of this vital material. A similar situation pertains in the supply of a number of other materials that are locally produced - such as aggregates, bricks, tiles, limestone and timber; and in cases where there is a local monopoly of supply, production levels are set to maximise revenues, keeping price above average costs. In addition, the poor and inconsistent quality of many locally-produced materials may result in a tendency to over-design, or in low quality of the finished project with high subsequent maintenance costs.

As a result of all of the factors listed above - as well as the limited availability of capital, inadequate equipment, and poorly developed transportation network - the construction industry in the majority of developing countries must be, by any definition, 'inefficient', with low levels of productivity and high costs. Also, cost-keeping standards themselves leave much to be desired, with many contractors knowing only if they have made a profit or loss on a project - and some not even knowing that. 'Without good cost records, and with inadequate management tools, it is unrealistic to expect that the quality/cost ratio can be assessed, let alone improved'.[32] Thus even where construction projects are implemented, all too often the cost is higher than anticipated, aggravating the financial constraint to the execution of development plans. The outlines of a solution to the many problems confronting the construction industry in developing countries, as well as the impediments which must be overcome before any such solution may be implemented, will form the subject of the next chapter.

NOTES

1. Such was the case for example in Ghana in 1965 and 1974, Uganda in 1965, Kenya in 1967, Nigeria in 1970 and Tanzania in 1968.

2. A 40 per cent to 60 per cent rise in the costs of the IBRD/IDA school-building programme was registered by the Ministry of Education. Similar complaints, involving price increases of between 25 per cent and 50 per cent, were raised by other public-sector bodies responsible for the execution of construction programmes.

3. Republic of Kenya, Economic Survey (Government Printer, Nairobi, 1967).

4. For the full report see E.J. Wells and E.R. Rado, 'Constraints and Costs in the Kenya Building Industry' Staff Paper no. 22 (Institute for

Development Studies, University of Nairobi, 1968.

5. For each of the 248 contracts awarded the following data was obtained: (1) the actual number of tenders submitted for any one contract (2) the number of firms invited to tender who failed to do so (3) the price variation on tenders submitted - higher price variations being taken as an indication of a lack of serious interest on the part of a number of the firms tendering and (4) delays in the execution of the work after contracts were awarded. It was thought that any or all of these variables might be adopted as possible indicators of the development of physical constraint on the implementation of construction projects. Contracts analysed comprised all those awarded by public-sector clients and all large contracts in the private sector.

6. The way in which the population, from which the sample was drawn, was established is described in detail in Wells and Rado, 'Kenya Building Industry'.

7. There were three officially-recognised grades of craftsmen in Kenya; entry to each of the grades was dependent upon passing the equivalent trade test.

8. The East African Region is generally understood to comprise the three adjacent countries of Kenya, Uganda and Tanzania. A number of services were shared between the three countries in colonial times. After independence an attempt was made to attain closer economic cooperation through the development of a common market, known as the East African Community. The Community was subject to increasing political strains, however, as the three countries embarked upon quite different development paths; it finally collapsed in the early 1970s.

9. For a detailed account of the production and marketing of quarry products see E.J. Wells, 'The Production and Marketing of Ballast in Kenya', Miscellaneous Paper no. 8 (Institute for Development Studies, University of Nairobi, 1969).

10. Many people in Kenya at the time mistakenly believed the cause of inadequate production and exploitative prices in the quarrying industry to lie in the fact that all the quarries were owned by Asians; they therefore proposed a policy of 'Africanisation' to overcome the problem. Investigation clearly showed, however, that the situation arose from the exercise of monopoly power by producers, rather than from their nationality; it was concluded that, if African quarry-owners were

encouraged to replace Asians, there was no reason to suppose they would behave in any different way.

11. Of the total average price increase in 1967 of 25 per cent or 30 per cent, 5 per cent was found to be due to a general increase in administered prices throughout the economy, 11 per cent was due to the increased cost of skilled labour, and 9.5 per cent to increase in materials prices. With additional indirect costs to the contractor caused by decreased availability of certain materials and skills, it seems unlikely that much of the increase in tender prices could be due to increased contractor profits, see Wells and Rado, 'Kenya Building Industry'.

12. This prognosis was borne out by subsequent events ... competition in the tender market continued at a high level, in fact actually increased following the entry of a number of new Asian firms which had been excluded by the licensing system from operating in other areas of the economy; but problems regarding the availability of materials and components intensified; prices of both materials and skilled labour continued to rise and quality of work to fall, see chapter six.

13. See M. Bienefeld, 'The Construction Industry in Tanzania', Economic Research Bureau Paper No. 69.4 (University of Dar-Es-Salaam, 1969).

14. This is known as the Mwananchi Engineering and Contracting Company or "MECCO". A full description of its history and analysis of its role in the development of construction resources in Tanzania will be found in chapter seven.

15. Foreign-exchange costs are generally higher on projects undertaken by foreign contracting firms, not only because of the large profit element which is usually transmitted out of the country, but also because such firms tend to employ a higher percentage of foreign personnel and to use techniques of construction that are far more capital-intensive.

16. See Ministry of Works, Local Construction Industry (Ministry of Works, Tanzania, 1977).

17. The problem of productivity is highlighted by the fact that costs of construction in Tanzania are level with those prevailing in Europe, while wages are significantly lower. Thus a 'staff house' in Tanzania might cost approximately the same as a similar house in Europe, despite lower wages, poorer quality and standards of equipment. See Ministry of Works, Local Construction Industry Study, p.96.

18. In Tanzania the problem was mainly of skilled men leaving the industry, for lack of adequate remuneration and/or career prospects. Elsewhere there may well be problems of their leaving the country for more rewarding opportunities in the construction industry abroad, either in neighbouring countries (e.g. Ghanaians migrating to Nigeria), or more distant parts (Far-Easteners working in the Middle East).

19. It should be noted that the situation regarding imported items was unnecessarily complicated by a complete absence of standardisation. For example, there were three different and non-compatible standards for imported electrical equipment. The state agency responsible for the importation of building materials (BHESCO) was in fact importing more than 8,000 items.

20. The case is well argued in the Ministry of Works, Local Construction Industry Study.

21. A series of factors contributed to this situation, e.g. the second round of oil price increases, the continued adverse trend in the terms of trade, a succession of bad harvests and the Ugandan war.

22. In the former category were wire products; steel nails, screws and bolts; plywood, chipboard, hardboard and flush doors; plastic pipes and fittings. The latter category included paints, corrugated iron and aluminium roofing sheets and rolled steel items, see Barker and Barton, 'The Construction Industry in Tanzania - The Current Situation, November 1980', Barker and Barton, quantity surveyors and construction cost consultants, Tanzania Ltd.

23. Profits and overheads were estimated at anything upwards of 35 per cent of the contract price. For this information I am grateful to Brian Barton of Barker and Barton, Tanzania Ltd.

24. See E.J. Wells, Expansion of Public-Sector Construction in Tanzania (National Construction Council, Dar-Es-Salaam, 1984).

25. For a full account of the situation in the construction industry in Ghana see G. Ofori, 'The Construction Industries of Developing Countries: The Applicability of Existing Theories and Strategies for their Improvement and Lessons for the Future: The Case of Ghana', unpublished Ph.D thesis, University of London, 1980. A much abbreviated account appears in G.A. Edmonds and D.W.J. Miles, Foundations for Change: Aspects of the Construction

Industry in Developing Countries (Intermediate Technology Publications, 1984).

26. See S. Ganeson, 'The Construction Industry in Sri-Lanka', World Employment Programme Research Working Paper No. 2-22/WP.90 (International Labour Office, Geneva, 1982); a shortened version also appears in Edmonds and Miles, Foundations for Change.

27. See Olu Falae 'The Challenge Facing the Construction Industry'; V.P. Diejomach, 'Government and the Construction Industry in Nigeria'; Akin Ogumpola 'The Structure of Building Costs and the Implications for Economic Development'; all appearing in Nigerian Economic Society, The Construction Industry in Nigeria, (University of Ibadan, 1974).

28. For a broad survey of the situation see UNCHS, Review of the Role and Contribution of the Construction Industry in Socio-Economic Growth in Developing Countries', Report of the Executive Director of UNCHS to the Fourth Session of the Commission on Human Settlements, HS/C/4/3 (UNCHS, Nairobi, 1981).

29. See Edmonds and Miles, Foundations for Change. It is also interesting to note that with professional fees amounting to as much as 15 per cent of the total cost of a contract, the loss of foreign-exchange due to the use of expatriate professional personnel may in fact amount to almost as much as the loss due to the use of imported materials, see Bienefeld, 'The Construction Industry in Tanzania'.

30. See, for example, ILO, 'Construction Skills', CIRF Monograph No. 4 (International Labour Office, Geneva, 1969).

31. For a synopsis of the problems confronting indigenous building contractors see Charles Cockburn, 'Nigerian Building Contractors: Practices, Problems and Needs', Building for Development, Research Paper No. 1 (Building for Development, London, 1970).

32. See UNIDO, 'Construction Industry', Monographs on Industrial Development No. 2 (United Nations, New York, 1969).

Chapter Four

BARRIERS TO DEVELOPMENT

Previous chapters have shown a major problem confronting the construction industry in developing countries to be the under-development of indigenous resources, both human and material. A solution would therefore seem to lie in the development of such resources, in both the qualitative as well as the quantitative sense, through the initiation of efficient and effective training programmes, and a massive programme of investment in the production and marketing of building materials. In addition, plans may be laid to secure improvements in the transport and distribution network, in the flow of finance and in the availability of plant and equipment for the construction sector. Providing such measures are taken, it may be argued that with sufficient investment, time and a favourable economic climate, the issue of supply inadequacy in the construction sector will be resolved.

Reality is not so simple, however, and knowledge of the industry leads one to be less sanguine. Also despite several Far Eastern models, a favourable economic climate would appear to many developing countries today to be little more than a 'pipe-dream'. During the early 1980s several developing countries were suffering from declining levels of per capita GDP, falling standards of living, and increasing balance of payment difficulties. In all but a handful of these countries such difficulties seem likely to persist. Thus a solution to the problem of inadequate resources in the construction sector must be sought within the limits imposed by strict foreign-exchange and other constraints.

In this connection, it should be noted that most developing countries have to date followed a policy of import substitution in the building materials industry. In practice this frequently means the establishment of local industries to produce materials identical to those previously imported - a process that may be termed 'import reproduction'. The local reproduction of previously imported materials and components generally means that raw materials used in the production process continue to be imported, as does the machinery and equipment which usually are capital-intensive and require large quantities of (imported) fuel, spare parts and technical assistance for operation and servicing. Sometimes only the finishing touches of the production process are carried out locally, such as the rolling and bending of bars from imported steel or the mixing of paint from imported chemicals. Hence the local production of building materials in developing countries has all too often amounted to little more than the substitution of one kind of imported material for another, with little use of local labour or development of locally-available raw materials and a subsequent collapse of the industry when the imported materials are no longer available.[1]

As an alternative to import reproduction, building materials industries need to be developed from locally-available raw materials, local sources of energy, and using locally-produced items of plant and equipment. There is no doubt that in the majority of countries such alternative industries do already exist. In fact a substantial amount of the building materials that are currently utilised for the production of basic shelter and related infrastructure (bricks, blocks, stone etc.), in both rural and urban areas, are produced in small-scale units using indigenous resources that are cheap and abundant. Some of these materials are produced in what has come to be known as the 'informal sector'; others in small workshops or factories. The production process is frequently under-capitalised and the product may be of low, and certainly of variable, quality. Nevertheless, these industries are already meeting the need for shelter for the vast majority of the population in most developing countries; and they are able to do this with little consumption of scarce resources of capital or foreign-exchange and with a high generation of employment. Given the objective of greater development of local resources, within the constraint of very limited availability of foreign-exchange, then the case for developing, improving and building upon this productive base can hardly be ignored.[2]

The point is well illustrated by a study of the construction industry in Sri-Lanka, which notes the high import-content of local materials industries and the need for a change to an alternative technology for at least a part of the construction programme, if output targets for the construction sector are to be met within the existing foreign-exchange constraint.[3] In an earlier work, S. Ganeson suggested that in Sri Lanka the pattern of demand in the construction section might be restructured along the following lines:

(1) Almost complete abandonment of the use of steel, cement, asbestos cement etc. in housing;
(2) The construction of modern houses, including 'luxury' houses, in bricks and tiles;
(3) An increase in the share of mud and tile houses;
(4) An increase in the share of conventional brick structures in non-residential construction;
(5) A reduction in the number of hardware items produced by the state hardware corporation (using capital-intensive technology) and an increase in production by the small-scale sector;
(6) The replacement of plastic and cast-iron pipes by concrete and earthenware;
(7) The use of local raw materials in the production of paint;
(8) An increase in electrical fittings and accessories from the small-scale sector;
(9) Curtailment of the use of heavy construction equipment.[4]

This list does not of course apply equally to all countries; and there is little point in attempting to economise on the use of foreign-exchange or capital if this can only be done at excessive cost. Nevertheless if such, or similar measures were to be adopted, not only would there be a chance of achieving output targets for the construction sector without undue additional strain on the balance of payments, but also considerable additional employment would be created locally. Such a move must, however, be accompanied by an efficient programme of training in the new techniques of materials production, as well as in new craft and supervisory skills for the construction industry.

Training is in fact a vital element of any programme to expand and improve upon the use of local resources in the construction sector. Because construction is a relatively labour-intensive industry, the quality of the local labour force will determine to a very large extent the quality and cost of the final product. But here again a solution is not so easily seen or so straightforward as it might at first sight appear. For while the need for training at all levels in the construction industry (to expand the supply of craftsmen, machine operators, technicians, supervisors, managers and professionals) is obvious, the means of attaining this objective are not. There are in fact enormous difficulties in the way of instituting effective training programmes in an industry where training 'on-the-job' is particularly important but where output levels fluctuate from year to year, and from month to month; where labour is still employed at casual, daily rates; and where competitive tendering for individual contracts on a 'one-off' basis is the normal way of organising the work. In addition there is the very real problem of retaining labour, once trained, within the industry and within the state - a problem that is particularly severe in, but by no means confined to, countries bordering on the middle-east or other oil-rich regions.

In view of these difficulties in setting-up effective training programmes, an alternative or complementary approach might be to attempt to adapt construction designs and technology in line with the level of skills that actually exists. Hence it is suggested that the specification of buildings and other structures should be such as to *not* require for efficient construction a level of skills that is not generally available. 'High-quality' or 'luxury' buildings requiring sophisticated craft skills are not really essential to the development of any economy and their buyers should not be subsidised by others. Plans might instead be based to a large extent upon a limited number of simple, standard building types, requiring only the repetition of a few simple operations on-site. Not only would such a move greatly facilitate the training problem, it would also simplify the problem of supervision, lead to a rapid improvement in the productivity of labour, as well as drastically reduce the requirements for scarce and expensive design skills.

It is therefore suggested that there are two aspects to a solution to the problem of supply in the construction industry in developing countries: (1)

the expansion and strengthening of the resources of manpower and materials available locally; (2) the achievement of a more efficient utilisation of the resources that currently exist, through a change in the technology of construction. The second of these two aspects is perhaps even more important than the first and has certainly been receiving an increasing amount of attention in recent years.[5] The key, however, to the attainment of both of these objectives, and particularly the second, lies in careful control over the design of structures; for it is the decisions taken at the briefing and design stage of the construction process that have the greatest impact upon the requirements for material inputs, the choice of techniques to be employed, the level of skills required and hence upon the final cost and speed of construction. Thus the design of buildings and other construction facilities should be very carefully thought through in order that the contractor may, in producing the building, make the most economical use of the skills, materials and equipment that are in short supply. Designs should be such as to facilitate the fullest possible development and use of local material products, based upon locally available resources and they should be closely geared to the skills that are available to carry them out. Only in this way may the full productive potential of local resources be released. That this kind of development in design is unlikely to materialise of its own accord will, however, be immediately apparent upon closer examination of the structure of the construction industry.

THE STRUCTURE OF THE CONSTRUCTION INDUSTRY

In a number of developing countries, particularly in Africa, the construction industry is still organised in the same way as that of the former colonial power prior to independence. The main outlines of this industrial structure have already been sketched in chapter one. Of major significance is the division of responsibility among the various participants in the construction process and the fact that although performing what are essentially complementary activities, they belong to quite separate commercial units. These separate commercial entities (design or engineering partnerships, professional surveyors, contractors, subcontractors and suppliers of materials and components) relate to each other by means of contracts. Relations between them are hierarchical (with sequential intervention of the participants) and generally temporary (with the dissolution of the construction team upon the completion of every project).

The most obvious implication of such an industrial structure, with its divided responsibilities, is that the construction industry becomes an arena for conflict, with the proliferation of legal suits and arbitrations among various interested parties - clients, professions, contractors or suppliers. That such disputes are time-consuming and costly (in terms of both money and personnel) and can be ill-afforded by developing countries, is beyond dispute. But even more serious than the legal implications is the effect of the industrial structure upon the cost and efficiency of the total construction process. Two aspects will be singled out for examination: (1) the effects of the divorce of the responsibility for design from the responsibility for production and (2) the uncertainty engendered by the use of a system of competitive tendering for individual construction projects.

THE DIVORCE OF DESIGN FROM PRODUCTION IN THE CONSTRUCTION PROCESS

The first and most obvious effect of the divorce of design from production in the construction process is that it has led to a certain amount of isolation of the professionals from technical developments in the construction industry, a fact which is reinforced by the rigid compartmentalisation of training. Consequently, the product may well be designed without sufficient knowledge of construction, or of alternative construction materials and techniques. The problem is compounded in African countries by the fact that the majority of private professional practices, as well as many posts in public-sector design departments, are still staffed by expatriates, or by local architects who were trained abroad. Their outlook, knowledge and experience of the construction process is therefore closely related to the conditions prevailing in industrialised countries; knowledge of local conditions and resources, particularly outside of the capital city, is scant. Furthermore, even where local schools of architecture or engineering have been opened in the developing countries themselves, these also tend to be staffed, of necessity, by professionals whose experience lies mainly in the industrialised countries. No doubt attempts are made to come to terms with local conditions. But teaching methods still tend to be based on those prevailing in more developed countries and little time appears to be spent in trying to understand the measures required for the development of resources in the construction sector in the third world, or in actually working on a construction site.[6] Indeed, in the opinion of the Secretary of State for Physical Planning in Mozambique, there is no school of architecture in existence today whose curriculum reflects the real needs of African countries.

The divorce of design from production in the construction process also means that the architect or engineer is isolated from a knowledge of actual production costs and of the costs of production based upon alternative designs. While it is often supposed that the role of the quantity surveyor has developed in such a way as to fill this gap in knowledge, such is not in fact the case. The main function of the quantity surveyor is to draw up a 'bill of quantities' to enable contractors to estimate their total tender price in such a way that he can check that the prices quoted are not absurd, and to subsequently measure any variation in the work in order to make payments to the contractor. In Britain and all former British colonies, finished units of work are measured according to the Standard Method of Measurement (SMM). Under the SMM the work is not divided for measurement purposes according to the way in which it is actually carried out on site; and the form of the bills is not designed to enable comparative cost analysis of different ways of designing a building to be made.[7] Also, the actual rates or prices which contractors quote include some margin for overheads and profits and these margins may be assigned indiscriminately to different parts of the work. For example, the trades occurring in the early stages of a contract are normally over-priced because an excess profit at this stage will reduce the amount of working capital that a contractor needs to employ during the contract. Finally, it should be noted that the 'bill of quantities' can in certain situations become a protective document, in the sense that if a designer has failed to complete his documentation before the bill is prepared (which so often is the case) or if the quantity surveyor knows that a certain architect or client is prone to vary the working during construction, he builds in a hidden 'contingency' by inflating the quantity of work in some areas to try to ensure that the final account figure does not exceed the tender price. One element in the contractor's competitiveness is his ability to identify these areas of over-measurement and under-value them, thereby reducing the amount of contingency and at the same time increasing his profit on the work that is actually carried out. Thus the quantity surveyor has no knowledge of the actual costs of construction but only of the prices quoted by contractors.[8] The development of the independent profession of quantity surveying, far from filling the gap in the architect's knowledge of construction costs has in fact enabled designers to neglect proper study of estimating and forced contractors to estimate and record costs in an unrealistic way. It has therefore imposed a considerable barrier to any movement towards cost reduction through experimentation in design. To put it another way, designs are not made in full cognisance of the effect of design and layout on costs. Consequently designs are often 'inefficient' in the sense that they require the use of more labour, materials and/or other resources than is really necessary to achieve their objective.

Communications and the transfer of knowledge between the various specialists in the construction industry is made even more difficult by the fact that the relationship between them is essentially hierarchical. The architect or engineer is the first to be appointed by the client and thereafter the relationship between him and the other participants tends to be that of employer to employed. Thus an architect designs a building (i.e. the spatial layout and overall plan) and then calls upon an engineer to design the structure; the possibility that the engineer's knowledge of structures might have suggested a more economical or more efficient plan is not considered. Similarly by the time that the design complete with the engineer's contribution has reached the builder there is no opportunity for the builder's knowledge to influence it. Information is only passed downwards, never in the reverse direction. As a result the incentive to experiment with new methods or materials is stifled. For it is the contractor who carries the risks and responsibility for construction; it is therefore the contractor who has the incentive to innovate - and yet he has no control over design, where the crucial decisions affecting materials, techniques and costs are taken. Thus, 'As long as design is divorced from the responsibility for building, the builder has practically no say in the opportunities or occasions for introducing, or making use of, innovations except to some extent in the technical organisation of the actual building process. Even in this limited field he can be seriously hampered by the unsuitability of designs for the use of new site techniques and equipment.'[9] The backwardness of the British building industry, at a time of almost unparalleled advance in science and technology in other fields, is attributed largely to this one fact.[10]

Finally, analysis of the relationships between the various participants in the construction process would be incomplete without brief reference to what is perhaps the most remarkable feature of this system - the fact that professional fees in the construction industry are generally calculated as a percentage of the final cost of the contract. Thus, not only do professionals not have the knowledge and experience required to research and develop the kind of designs that are so urgently needed, under the existing structure of professional fees they also have no incentive. Given that the objective of a private professional practice or design office is to maximise returns with a minimum of expenditure, it is surely not too cynical to suggest that an organisation might operate as follows:

(1) Attempt to interpret the client's requirements in the most expensive terms likely to be accepted. In most developing countries no standards have been laid down for government buildings; most clients have little idea of what they really need and even less of what they can realistically expect to obtain. It is therefore left very much to the architect or engineer to interpret their requirements for them. If the estimated costs exceed the funds available then the usual reaction of the public-sector client is either to request additional funds or to allow the project to go ahead in anticipation that, once it is committed, government will be obliged to finance it.[11]

(2) To avoid contracts involving the development or use of standard designs for components or building types, as this has to be carried out on a reduced fee-scale. The beneficial effect of the use of standard designs on productivity and training is mentioned above.

(3) To avoid projects with a high research content, such as low-cost housing or buildings based on a new structural technique or alternative materials, as these are the projects upon which it is difficult to show a good return. They are, of course, exactly the kinds of projects to be encouraged if the objective of increased efficiency through the use of appropriate technology is to be achieved.

Under circumstances such as these, it is almost inevitable that the designs that are adopted in developing countries should be based upon the technology, unadapted, of the developed industrialized world. The result (given the weakness of the local industry) is structures that are high-cost, subject to over-runs, low quality and often late in completion. Local resources of materials remain undeveloped and local labour untrained.

THE SYSTEM OF COMPETITIVE TENDERING

In addition to the separation of design from construction, the majority of developing countries with market economies have copied from the advanced nations the practice of competitive tendering in the award of contracts. This means that either all contractors (in the case of an 'open tender') or a number of specially-selected firms (in the case of 'selective tender') are invited, after the designs have been essentially completed, to submit a price for which they will undertake to complete the whole of the work involved in construction. The bid may be in the form of a 'lump sum', estimated on the basis of close scrutiny of the drawings and the specification; or it may be in the form of an agreed 'schedule of rates' or a priced 'bill of quantities', whereby provision is made for re-measurement of each item of work as the construction proceeds. Whatever the particular form of tendering procedure adopted, it is widely believed that this kind of competition between contracting firms is essential in order to provide a spur to efficiency in the construction industry and to safeguard the interests of the client, or consumer.

It is, however, extremely doubtful whether the particular kind of competition that has become the norm in the construction industry in developing countries does in fact offer all of the advantages claimed for it. First it has already been noted that there is not one tender market in developing countries but several. The level of competition existing between the much smaller number of firms operating in any one sub-division of the market must therefore be much less than anticipated; competition for particular types of structure may in fact be more illusory than real and sometimes not even that. But even where some degree of competition for individual contracts does exist, it is important to remember that the design is already fixed and that the time taken to complete the job and the quality of workmanship are seldom evaluated; so that the sole basis on which firms compete is the price alone. Furthermore, the price submitted is only an estimate, or a guess on the part of the contractor of the probable cost to himself (allowing for some element of profit) for completing the work. Thus, the firm that wins the contract is simply the one submitting the lowest estimate - which is not necessarily, and not often, the one with the lowest actual costs or the highest level of efficiency. In an industry with no significant barriers to entry it is all too easy for new and inexperienced firms to win contracts through the submission of low bids; the way in which they subsequently carry out (or do not carry out) the work may leave much to be desired. Also, it is all too easy for a contractor to submit a low bid, knowing that certain items of work in the bill of quantities have been over-measured or that hidden sums of money will be made available by a 'friendly' client in order to inflate the final tender sum. In other words it is just too easy to 'cheat' in the tendering game and this is especially so in developing countries.

Thus, the alleged benefits of competition in the construction industry should not be over-stated. It does not automatically rule out corruption. Neither does it necessarily provide an incentive to efficiency among contracting firms, or ensure the survival of the fittest. The most that can be claimed is that competitive tendering may sometimes give a client a better price on an individual contract, especially when the industry is slack or the market keen. On the other hand the negative effects of requiring contractors to compete for each contract on a 'one-off' basis may in the long run outweigh any immediate advantages to the individual client. For competitive tendering reduces even further the possibility of cooperation between designer and contractor, as the contractor is only appointed after the designs are complete. In fact 'competitive tendering (for the production of a given design) amounts to neglecting the contribution that the production team could make to design, and ignoring the skills, plant and equipment that they may use in achieving the objective. It presents therefore the risk of freezing technological progress in so far as it works satisfactorily only within well-accepted, and therefore conventional, procedures and techniques.'[12]

Further, competitive tendering for individual contracts means the dissolution of the 'building team' after each contract is complete. Hence the development of continuous working relationships between the various participants in the construction process is impossible. In particular, there is less chance for the contractor's experience of production on one project to be used to obtain a better performance on the next. Even more serious, the contractor has no idea of the size, nature or location - or even the existence - of his future work-load, and is therefore inhibited from making any investments whose benefits would only accrue in the longer term. This means that he is inhibited from developing local resources of materials, from investing in plant and machinery, from stabilising the labour force and training local labour, from keeping accurate records of costs, or from experimenting with alternative innovative techniques within the areas of decision-making that *are* under his control - all of which investments are of course vital in developing countries for stimulating the development of the local construction and building materials industries and achieving more economic building in the longer term. In short, competitive tendering in the construction industry creates uncertainty, and destroys the incentive to invest. It inhibits the stabilisation of the labour force, and thus serves to perpetuate a low wage/low productivity spiral. Thus, while it may appear to ensure a relatively low and honest price for an individual contract, it has very serious negative effects upon the overall level of investment and productivity in the construction industry as a whole.

SUMMARY AND CONCLUSIONS

It may be concluded that the emergence of both superficial and more fundamental solutions to the problems confronting the construction industry in developing countries - the more effective development, and the better utilisation, of existing resources - are themselves seriously constrained by the structure of the industry; in particular by the separation of responsibility for design from the responsibility for production and the competitive tendering system. These problems of inhibiting contractual relationships and industrial structure are not just in theory a subject for reform; they have in fact been the cause of concern in developed market economies for a number of years. In Britain this concern has given rise to a number of government-sponsored, or government-supported, enquiries and reports - the general conclusion of which is that the industrial structure is inconsistent with the most efficient use of resources, or with high productivity, in the construction industry.[13] Change is slow to come, due to a very large extent to professional vested interest and client (particularly public-sector client) conservatism. But certain changes have occurred. Professional fee-scales have been revised and competition between professionals on fees allowed; the barriers to cooperation between architects and contractors have been lowered, with an increasing number of 'joint ventures' or 'package deals'; and in some sections of the market the 'negotiation' of contracts is gradually replacing the practice of competitive tendering.[14] In the USA these changes have proceeded much faster, and progressed much further, than in Britain. In the private sector, negotiated contracts and package deals are now more common than competitive tendering; fees are lower than they are in Britain; and restrictive practices among professionals far less.[15] For these and other reasons, productivity has been found to be significantly higher, costs lower and progress faster, in the construction industry in the USA than in the UK.[16]

Unfortunately such changes occurring in the construction industries of the advanced industrial nations have not been mirrored in all countries of the third world. Many of the poorest and least developed countries in Africa, Asia and Latin America (as well as some that are not so poor) still follow the most traditional and somewhat inhibiting contractual practices evolved in Europe and North America in the last century. And yet it is here that the need to find some solution to the problem is most urgent. One hopes that in attempting to develop some more appropriate industrial structure and more flexible contractual procedures, these countries will not fall into the trap of attempting to copy blindly the changes now taking place in the developed market economies - where many of the solutions adopted are dependent upon the existence of a large, highly-developed and competitive private construction sector with well-developed infrastructure and support systems. The poorest countries must seek to find new and innovative forms and institutions for a fundamental re-structuring of their construction industries, in order to release their productive potential. In such attempts, indigenous resources must clearly play a prominent role as much also, in the absence of a developed private sector, the government. The role of governments in the construction process and the kind of actions they might take will be examined in the next chapter.

NOTES

1. For example in Tanzania 57 per cent of the cost of locally-produced cement is made up of imported components while for the local production of reinforcing steel, rails, asphalt and roofing sheets all raw materials and components are imported, see A.L. Mtui 'The Exploitation, Use and Development of Indigenous Building Materials in Tanzania' in National Construction Council, Seminar on Building Materials (National Construction Council, Dar-Es-Salaam, 1982). Ganeson has noted a similar situation in Sri-Lanka with all raw material requirements for the steel and hardware industries and 80 per cent of those for the plywood industry imported, see S. Ganeson 'The Construction Industry in Sri-Lanka', World Employment Programme Research Working Paper No. WEP 2-22/WP.90 (International Labour Office, Geneva, 1982).

2. See E.J. Wells, 'The Small-Scale Production of Indigenous Building Materials in Developing Countries', report for UNCHS, June 1984.

3. The average import-content of local building materials production was found to be 35 per cent to 40 per cent of the total cost, increasing to 100 per cent in the case of steel products, see Ganeson, 'The Construction Industry in Sri-Lanka'.

4. S. Ganeson, 'Employment Generation through Investment in Housing and Construction', unpublished Ph.D thesis, University of London, 1976.

5. See for example United Nations 'Research and Development Projects for detailed discussion:

Building Technologies for Developing Countries', Report of the Secretary General to the Eighth Session of the Committee on Housing Building and Planning, E/C.6/137 (United Nations Centre for Housing, Building and Planning, New York, 1973); W.P. Strassmann, 'Building Technology and Employment in the Housing Sector of Developing Countries' World Employment Programme Research Working Paper, WEP 2-22 (International Labour Office Geneva, 1975); UNIDO 'Appropriate Technology for Construction and Building Materials', Monographs on Appropriate Technology No. 12, ID/232/12 (United Nations Industrial Development Organisation, Vienna, 1980); CIB/RILEM, Appropriate Building Materials for Low-Cost Housing (E. & F. Spon, London and New York, 1983).

6. A notable exception is Cuba, see chapter eight.

7. Experiments have been taking place over a number of years into the development of alternative types of bills of quantities. Of the three major variations developed to date - elemental bills, occupational bills and activity bills - the last corresponds most directly to the way in which work is actually organised on the construction site and therefore holds the greatest promise. Their introduction is hampered however by conservatism, as well as professional vested interest on the part of the quantity surveyors.

8. Quantity surveyors would of course deny this to be the case; many have in fact actually set themselves up as professional 'cost consultants'.

9. M. Bowley, The British Building Industry : Four Studies in Response and Resistance to Change (Cambridge University Press, Cambridge, 1966) p.444.

10. Ibid.

11. This paragraph is based upon the author's own experience as a senior economist in the Ministry of Planning, Tanzania.

12. UNIDO, 'Construction Industry', Monographs on Industrial Development, No. 2. (United Nations, New York, 1969).

13. See H. Emmerson, Survey of Problems before the Construction Industries (HMSO, London, 1962); H. Banwell, The Placing and Management of Contracts for Building and Civil-Engineering Works (HMSO, London, 1964); Tavistock Institute, Interdependence and Uncertainty (Tavistock Publications, London, 1966).

14. For further details of these alternative contractual arrangements see chapter 5.

15. See Building Design and Construction (December 1984) pp.57-121. For an explanation as to why projects are not used in the public-sector in the USA see Greenfield, 'Turnkey Construction in the United States', ASCE Journal of the Construction Division (1982) 108, pp.201-210.

16. See RICS, U.K. and its Construction Industries. A Comparison of Design and Contract Procedures (Royal Institute of Chartered Surveyors, 1979); B. Hill, 'Why Construction is Quicker and Cheaper in the USA', Chartered Surveyor, 112, (December 1979) pp.158-161; C. Gray and R. Flanagan 'US Productivity and Fast-Tracking Start on the Drawing Board', Construction Management and Economics (2) (Autumn 1984) pp.133-143.

Chapter Five

A ROLE FOR THE STATE

THE ROLE OF GOVERNMENTS IN THE CONSTRUCTION PROCESS

Governments in all countries have in principle the means at their disposal to exert a great deal of influence over activities in the construction sector. They may do this either *indirectly* through the imposition of legislative and planning controls or various monetary incentives, or *directly* through their involvement as client, designers, supervisor or producer in the construction process itself. Each of the possible alternative ways in which governments may secure some degree of control over the construction sector will be outlined in turn.

First, in all countries the state is responsible for the formulation of general economic and social policies and for the enactment and enforcement of legislation to encourage these policies to be carried out. Thus, governments can indirectly influence the construction process in both public and private sectors of the economy through the implementation of a wide range of fiscal and monetary policies that affect the construction sector. Examples of such policies might be the protection of local industries through the imposition of tariffs (or non-tariff barriers) on the importation of machinery, plant, equipment or building materials; the provision of incentives in the form of tax reliefs to the local contracting or building materials industries; or the stimulation of employment through the provision of subsidies on the use of labour.

In addition to general economic policies, the state may have a more direct influence upon the construction process in the public and private sectors through the enactment and enforcement of building codes and regulations and other types of planning control. The majority of construction projects, at least those in the formal sector of the economy, have to be based on plans that are submitted for approval to some kind of public authority. In many countries it is central government that is responsible for the elaboration and enforcement of planning, building and safety regulations; in others this function is delegated to regional, provincial or municipal authorities. But whoever is responsible, this represents in principal a very powerful means of control over construction activity in the formal sector.

Thirdly, governments may exercise even more direct control over the construction process through their role as clients of the construction industry. Central and local government building programmes in all countries, irrespective of their social, political and/or economic structure, account for a large proportion of total construction output; and there is a good deal of evidence to suggest that governments' role as client of the construction industry in developing countries is increasing. Thus, government responsibility for as much as 60 per cent of the total construction output is quite common; and in some countries the figure is even higher.[1] This comprises most of the construction investment outside of housing, as well as most of the formal sector low-cost housing activity. It should be noted in this connection, however, that 'government' does not necessarily mean one single identifiable public body; responsibility for the commissioning of construction projects may in fact be widely diffused throughout the public sector of the economy. The ministries most directly concerned are those responsible for transport and communications, defence, education, health and housing. In addition, local authorities frequently have their own construction programmes, as do also in some cases the nationalised sectors of the economy. Nevertheless, most countries do have one central government department (generally referred to as 'public works') which is responsible for a large part, if not the whole, of the central government building programmes, and usually the main network of public infrastructure (roads, bridges, harbours, airports) as well.

As clients of the construction industry, governments are clearly in a position to exercise a considerable amount of control over the type, location, standard, technology and method of execution of construction projects. This is so even if they commission the private construction industry for the actual execution of their construction programmes. In a number of countries, however, public-sector clients may exercise an even greater degree of control by assuming direct responsibility for the design of projects themselves and sometimes also for the production. Thus it is not uncommon in both developed and developing countries, even in market economies, to find a ministry of public works with its own 'in-house' designers, its own 'direct works' construction labour force and its own maintenance and repair teams - responsible for the design, production and maintenance of some part of the total public sector construction programme by force account. In some cases specialised ministries or departments of central government (usually ministries of education, or health) may assume direct responsibility for the maintenance of their own facilities and/or the design and construction of new works. And such 'direct works' design, construction and repair teams may even be found at local government level. Alternatively, governments may undertake design and construction work and the production of building materials or components through semi-autonomous 'national construction companies' or corporations. In either case, whether through direct works departments or 'parastatal' organisations, government control over construction work is both direct and pervasive.

It will be noted that the various ways in which governments may participate in, or exercise control over, the construction process have been described above as if they were ranked on some sort of continuous scale - from an interest that is diffused, general and indirect, to participation that is intensive, particular and direct. The points on such a scale are not necessarily sequential, however; thus, governments may be found to be actually involved in the production stage, whilst neglecting to formulate policy for the construction industry at the national level. Also, the degree and intensity of public-sector involvement in the production process is not necessarily related to political or ideological factors; it may have at least as much to do with the relative strength, or weakness, of the private sector and of competing Government Agencies. The point, however, is that governments can and do exert influence and control over the construction sector in a variety of ways and through a variety of means.

Most governments do in fact make some conscious effort to use this power of control to deal with some of the problems facing the construction sector.

For example, in most countries governments attempt to afford some degree of protection to the local construction and building materials industries through the imposition of import duties, quotas, etc. and in the provision of subsidies, often in the form of tax rebates, to local firms. Most governments also lend support, even if only nominally, to programmes for the training of local labour and for research into locally-produced building materials and components. Some may attempt to expand supply, increase competition and/or promote the development of a local industry through the establishment of one or more national construction companies, such as are found in Ghana, Syria or Tanzania. And a few examples may be found of governments which have adopted imaginative policies to control standards, or the technology of construction projects; to develop an indigenous private contracting industry through the up-grading of the informal sector; or to implement or improve upon planning and programming procedures for the sector as a whole. By and large, however, such instances are rare. Evidence would suggest that the vast majority of countries, both developing and industrialised, have not progressed very far in attempts to formulate and implement a coherent policy for the construction sector. It is the view of the United Nations Centre for Human Settlements (UNCHS), as expressed in its report to the fourth session of the Commission on Human Settlements, that even when concerted and intelligent efforts have been made, the results frequently appear to be disappointing.[2] This failure has been attributed to a number of factors - such as the inability of governments to appreciate the importance of construction; their failure to take a 'holistic' view of the construction process or to consider all aspects of construction in the light of overall national policies; or simply to the fact that efforts by governments to promote the construction industry have 'foundered in a sea of complex cause and effect relationships, extensive fragmentation of the industry, and its sensibilities to a wide range of issues and constraints.'[3] While not denying the validity of all of these factors, it may perhaps be worthwhile to enquire a little deeper into the reasons for governments' apparent ineffectiveness.

PROBLEMS IN POLICY IMPLEMENTATION

Undoubtedly the major stumbling block to the adoption of more effective policies for controlling the implementation of construction projects and the development of the construction sector must be found in the structure of the construction industry, as outlined in the previous chapter. In particular, the separation of design from production in the construction process and the remuneration of designers on the basis of a fixed percentage fee effectively means that there is no *overall incentive* within the structure of the construction industry towards an improvement in productivity or reduction in costs. This means that financial inducements such as subsidies on the use of labour or taxes on the use of imported equipment, while they may influence the way in which a contractor carries out a particular operation on-site (provided of course that this is not also prescribed at the design stage) are unlikely to have any significant effect upon the design of the project or upon the general technology that is used - and hence upon the intensity of use of labour as opposed to other factors of production. Likewise, the imposition of tariffs upon imported materials, or the provision of tax reliefs for local materials production may not serve to encourage the use of the local, as opposed to the imported, products - simply because designers (who have complete control over the materials that are used) do not have any direct incentive to specify the least cost alternative. At the same time, lack of control over design on the part of producers increases the level of uncertainty and therefore of risk involved in developing new sources of materials and hence results in a similar lack of responsiveness to financial incentives at the production stage. Thus, because of the separation of design and production processes, normal monetary incentives do not stimulate the expected response in the construction industry.

Moreover even when more direct, non-tariff controls are imposed upon the use of key factors of production, designers do not always immediately respond to the relative scarcity of certain items of materials or equipment, but frequently continue to specify products which are no longer available, with long delays in implementation as a result. Thus, in Tanzania in 1984 it was found that architects were continuing to accept (even actively solicit) briefs for projects which they knew could not possibly be built because government simply did not have the funds; and they were continuing to base their designs upon imported, hence unavailable, materials and components ... 'a situation which surely cannot be divorced from the fact that consultants are paid a percentage fee for their services, based upon the final cost of the project, and they are paid most of this fee before construction begins and whether or not it begins'.[4]

Neither do building and planning regulations (a more direct form of control over technology in the construction industry) generally work in the way that might be expected. For it is important to realise that the adoption of building standards and regulations in third world countries generally followed the spread of 'international' building materials and techniques from the advanced countries. Thus they were developed for application with sophisticated modern manufactured materials and components. As such they are totally inapplicable to the use of local building materials produced in small-scale units by largely manual processes which, with the lower strengths and uneven qualities, cannot meet the standard required. Consequently, in the enforcement of such regulations, locally-produced alternative materials are either banned from use in the controlled areas entirely, or extra steps are taken in the design of the structure to guarantee the quality of the finished product, irrespective of the quality of the individual components used - resulting in a substantial degree of 'over-design'. This has serious implications. For not only are these standards and regulations adopted in all public-sector construction programmes and for large private buildings in the major towns but an atempt is also sometimes made to apply similar standards on 'site and service' schemes. To the extent that such schemes are implemented, not only are the possibilities for the expansion of the market for the production of small-scale materials industries reduced, but the traditional market for these products (housing for the low-income earners) is also being eroded.[5]

Thus the enforcement of building regulations and planning controls in the statutory planning zones of developing countries all too often means, in practice, the imposition of unrealistically high standards and acts as a constraint on the more widespread development and use of locally-produced 'alternative' building materials. In the opinion of one author, current specifications used in Ghana have 'institutionalised the national over-dependence on imported constructional inputs'.[6] The lower propensity to consume the products of the informal building materials industries in Nairobi than in Kampala has also been attributed to the stronger enforcement of public controls (in the form of planning and building regulations) and the greater involvement of the public-sector in low-cost housing in the former city.[7]

What then of the alternative of lifting some restrictions and revising and adapting the regulations to take account of the characteristics and the potential of local materials? There is evidence that crippling restrictions have been lifted in a number of countries, for example, the eventual removal of restrictions on the use of 'landcrete' in Ghana. Also, building regulations and specifications can be, and have been, revised. Although a great deal of time and effort is required to actually produce revised regulations and specifications, based upon more appropriate standards and norms, it has been done in a number of countries, frequently with some international support.[8] But then the real problem arises of how to ensure that the revised regulations are actually adopted and enforced. In this connection it is useful to remember that building regulations are only guidelines; it is how they are applied in practice that is critical. And since all of the major decisions affecting the use of materials and labour in construction and the technology to be adopted are generally taken at the design stage, this will again depend to a very large extent upon the training, background, attitudes and above all the *interests* of designers. Design is the active ingredient in the equation; building regulations merely passive. Thus, changing regulations alone will achieve nothing unless the current bias of designers towards modern, sophisticated, highly capital-intensive products and processes is also changed.

Further difficulties arise when governments attempt to act to secure a more efficient construction sector through their role as clients of the industry. One of the most common objectives (and the type of action frequently espoused by experts and advisers in this field) is to attempt to stabilise demand in the construction sector. The 'ironing out' of the peaks and troughs in construction activity is in fact widely believed to be the most effective means to encourage the development of a more stable, more efficient and more productive industry. Yet not only is this an extremely difficult objective to achieve in any economy (especially so in poor countries which are heavily dependent upon taxes from unstable exports and the inflow of capital from abroad for major development projects) but the objective itself is perhaps misguided. For the stabilisation of output from the industry as a whole is neither a necessary nor a sufficient condition for the provision of continuity of demand for individual firms and continuous working relationships among a particular building team. It is these latter things that are needed in order to reduce uncertainty, stabilise the labour force, and create a better climate for investment within the construction sector. Here governments could clearly do more. They could in fact use their position as significant and on-going clients of the industry to secure both more continuous production and more stable working relationships among the various participants in the construction process. But in order to achieve this there must be significant changes in the way in which contracts are let. The process of design must be much more carefully controlled and the practice of competitive tendering for each individual contract abandoned in at least a part of the government's construction programme.

Finally, even when governments enter the construction field as producers (either designers or constructors) public-sector construction capacity is itself all too often closely modelled upon the structure of the private industry, with public-sector clients copying the most inhibiting practices of the private sector. Thus, public-sector designers are frequently exhorted to work more closely with the construction industry or to base their designs upon the resources that are actually available in developing countries. But they are all too often in practice carefully insulated from the 'rough and tumble' of construction activity in their sterilised design offices and put to work on the production of complex and sophisticated 'one-off' plans. Even if they have no direct financial incentive (such as exists among private sector designers) to spend their client's money, there is certainly no strong inducement to save it.

At the same time, public-sector construction units, with no control over designs, are instructed to behave as private sector contractors and make profits for the state, whilst competing with private-sector firms on each and every 'one-off' contract. This they clearly cannot do. The inability to complete in fact manifests itself in a number of ways and for a variety of reasons. First, a public-sector contractor cannot compete with the private sector in obtaining work, not because it is not competent (which is frequently only an excuse) but because it is not allowed to offer financial or other inducements to potential clients.[9] Secondly, it cannot compete for scarce skilled and experienced manpower because of restrictions on wages and conditions of employment in the public-sector. Thirdly, it cannot compete for material resources because it does not have the flexibility or the know-how to exploit the 'black market' (which in developing countries is often the only means of obtaining scarce items). And finally, it cannot compete for financial resources because of its lack of collateral and consequent inability to obtain loans and credit - a situation which is generally exacerbated by the poor record of payment of its (public-sector) clients. The most usual result of attempts to force a public-sector contractor to compete with the private sector is the gradual starvation of the former - in terms of contracts, labour, materials, equipment and funds - so that it may be eventually disbanded in disgust, apparently vindicating the views of economists, politicians and aid agencies alike about the 'inefficiency' of governments when they involve themselves in what many regard as the proper preserve of the private sector.[10] Far from using their influence to secure a more efficient and effective construction industry, governments' involvement in the construction sector, as producer, all too often ends up as a charade.

What then should governments in developing countries do in order to reduce their country's dependence upon imports in the construction sector? How can they ensure the development of a more responsive and more efficient construction industry, with a more appropriate technology at its base? All of the evidence appears to point in one direction ... that very little progress will be made towards the achievement of this objective unless, or until, governments are prepared to use their substantial power of control, as well as their direct involvement as client and producer in the construction process, to change the way in which contracts are let and eliminate some of the existing irrationalities in the structure of the industry. In particular, they must attempt to secure a restructuring of working relationships, embodying a more effective pattern of communications among the various participants (especially designers and producers) in the construction industry, as well as a more stable and secure environment for investment for the future. Only then will better designs, based upon a more appropriate technology and more developed and productive resources, develop. Some suggestions as to alternative ways in which this objective may be approached and some stumbling blocks likely to be enountered in the process, will be outlined in the last section of this chapter.

TOWARDS A MORE RATIONAL STRUCTURE

One immediately obvious contradiction in the organisation of the construction industry that is readily susceptible to government action is, of course, the structure of professional fees. The need for a revision in the basis for the calculation of professional fees, as well as in the actual fee scales that are used, has been apparent (indeed the subject of much discussion) for many years now, in a number of countries.[11] The irrationality of the traditional structure of fee-scales has, in fact, finally been conceded by that most conservative of bodies, the Royal Institute of British Architects; and some greater degree of rationality (including a degree of competition on price, or 'fee-cutting') has finally been allowed to intrude into the design process in Britain. Unfortunately this is not yet the case in a number of developing countries, at least those with which the author is most familiar, where fee-cutting is not allowed and where professional fees are still calculated as a fixed percentage of the final contract sum. Quite apart from the effect of such a method of remuneration upon the type of designs that materialise, a secondary but not unimportant consideration is the actual level of fees - which frequently amounts in total to as much as 15 per cent of the cost. While this may be reasonable for complex and sophisticated structures involving a large number of specialised services, it is certainly not reasonable for simple structures requiring only the services of a designer and surveyor. Furthermore, with a large number of private professionals operating in the third world being non-residents or non-citizens of the countries that give them work, such fees (representing quite substantial sums of money) are generally remitted straight back out of the country, doing little to alleviate the problem of balance of payments constraint. One wonders whether the poorest countries in the third world can really afford to offer such 'rich pickings' to the excess professional manpower of the more developed nations and for how long they will continue to do so. There is no doubt that a more rational and certainly a more just basis for professional remuneration can and must be developed.

It is in fact possible to conceive of a fee-scale that would not only remove the disincentive but actually offer some positive incentive to develop designs that should eventually result in a much lower cost of construction. For instance, strong financial inducements could be offered for the development of standard details, for each additional opportunity for repetition of products or processes within a design, for research into new techniques, or for the development of designs suitable for use with alternative building materials. In addition to the incentive to develop more appropriate designs, however, architects and engineers must be afforded an opportunity to involve themselves more closely in the production process, so that they can begin to improve upon their knowledge of construction costs and techniques and hence place themselves in a stronger position to be able to evaluate alternatives. Thus, the revision of fee-scales and the provision of financial incentives (which are only partial in their application), although a step in the right direction, is not a sufficient condition for real progress. It is to a reconstruction of working relationships throughout the whole construction process that one must look for any radical improvement in design and productivity in the industry.

As we have shown in the last chapter, departures from the traditional pattern of relationships in the building industry are by no means new. Speculative building by contractors, on the basis of their own designs; the production of pre-fabricated buildings, designed and erected on-site by the producer himself; 'turnkey projects', 'package deals', serial contracts, management contracts etc. have all been suggested and adopted at various times and places as solutions to the problem of effective integration between designers and producers in the construction industry.[12] Indeed some of these solutions have been with us for a very long time and may even pre-date the development of the general contractor and what has come to be regarded as the conventional system.[13] Two of these broad departures from the traditional pattern seem worthy of consideration in relation to the problem facing the majority of developing countries today. These are negotiated contracts, and the package deal.

The alternatives to competitive tendering in the construction industry are often grouped under the common heading of *negotiated contracts*. Under this common head, a great variety of procedures have been developed over the years in a number of countries to enable the client and the design team to associate contractors (and in some cases also the manufacturers of building materials and components) with the early stages of the decision-making process. The most beneficial of these would be an arrangement whereby a nominated contractor joins the 'design consortia' at the earliest possible stage; his knowledge of alternative materials and methods of construction is thereby made available to the design team; he may cooperate with architects and engineers in determining the techniques of production and the possible alternative materials that could be used and in developing and defining detailed plans and specifications. In this way, designers are able to make use of the accumulated experience of a contractor. The contractor, on the other hand, benefits from the development of a more workable and more rational (from the point of view of production) design. He also benefits from the fact that he has some advanced knowledge of the contract and can therefore to some extent plan ahead to ensure that his requirements of labour, materials and equipment are in fact met.

All of the benefits to be derived from the negotiation of contracts, and the early involvement of the contractor in the process of design are further enhanced, however, if such arrangements are extended over a number of contracts, as opposed to just one. If a number of similar contracts were to be made available in this way to the same design and construction team (known as 'serial contracts') then the experience gained on one project could be used to obtain a considerably improved performance, in terms of both design and construction, on the next. Furthermore, the contractor would have an assured programme of work and thus be in a much stronger position to make investments in materials, equipment and labour, the benefit of which might only be felt in the longer term. Consequently conditions are created for the possible emergence of a more efficient and more productive industry.

There are of course certain difficulties in the way of introducing negotiated contracts into the construction industry, particularly by public-sector clients. The most frequently raised objection is that if there is no competition for the construction of a contract, then the client has no means of telling whether or not the price quoted by the contractor is fair. This objection is undoubtedly valid. Although it should be noted that there is in any case no competition for design, under either this arrangement or more conventional practices, and no way of the client knowing whether he is getting good value for money from his design team. And yet this, strangely, does not seem to give cause for concern. Also, it has already been shown in chapter three that in some developing countries there is in practice little or no real competition among contractors; pretence to abide by it in these circumstances may be doing more harm than good to all concerned. Public accountability might perhaps be sought elsewhere. One suggestion is for contractors with whom the government negotiates to be asked to 'open their books' to the client and his advisers and negotiate a price based upon the actual costs of production, perhaps with any savings over and above the estimated price being split between the two. In this way it may be possible to ensure that some of the benefits arising from closer and more continuous working relationships between designers and producers are in fact passed on to the client.[14]

A more fundamental objection to the practice of negotiating large and repetitive contracts with private-sector contractors is that such a move may encourage market concentration in the construction industry, without necessarily leading to any fundamental re-structuring of capacity, increase in investment or improvement in production methods. G. Ive has argued that this has occurred in Britain.[15] On the other hand, experience in the USA, where negotiated contracts in the private sector are at least as common as competitive tendering and costs are well below the levels prevailing in the UK, would seem to tell a different story.[16]

On balance it would seem that in developing countries negotiated contracts might be used to advantage on some types of public-sector construction projects. In some countries governments are in fact finding that this is the only sensible way to proceed - especially where there is little or no competition in the industry, or when clients have to deal with a multitude of small, inexperienced indigenous contracters all vying with each other to obtain a contract in the public sector. Competition on price alone makes no sense whatever in these circumstances. Negotiation, on the other hand, presents an opportunity to encourage the better-organised and more promising firms through the offer of continuous work. Whether or not the potential benefits to be derived from negotiation are actually realised will depend to a large extent upon the strength of the client's team of technical advisers and their ability to talk on terms of equality with contractors. The advantages in this connection of channelling all public-sector projects through one body, such as a ministry of public works, where the technical resources of government may be concentrated, could be substantial.

Apart from the difficulties mentioned above, negotiated contracts do have one other serious limitation; that the origin of the initiative for design under such a system generally remains with the architect or engineer, who most commonly acts as the coordinator of the project and agent of the client. This is not the case with the 'package deal', where the traditional relationships in the construction industry are completely reversed. A package deal is in fact an arrangement whereby a contracting firm employs its own professional advisers and offers to take full responsibility for the whole construction process, from design right through to the delivery of the finished structure. The advantages of such an arrangement are immediately apparent. Because there is one unified responsibility to the client for all stages of the construction process, the client has only to deal with one organisation; the final cost is settled from the beginning, barring variations at the instigation of the client; and the various participants cannot shift responsibility, the architect to the builder and vice versa. Most important of all, the contractor benefits because the design is worked out in cooperation with all parties from the start, which means that it can be closely geared to both the contractor's capacity and the problems involved in the whole production process, from the preparation of the detailed drawings to the handing over of the finished structure. Moreover, where a number of different packages are offered by separate organisations in competition with one another (in which case the client defines only in very general terms the main features of the work to be achieved) there is for the first and only time in the construction industry genuine competition in both production *and* design. Small wonder that competitive package deals are considered by many to offer the best method so far evolved for achieving full integration of design and production and are put forward as a possible solution to the problems confronting the construction industry in the developed world.

What, however, of their applicability to developing countries? There are two serious disadvantages to such a system. First, when it is used in a competitive situation it is extremely wasteful of resources. In fact the time and cost involved in the production of designs for unsuccessful bids may in practice discourage firms, or consortia of designers and contractors, from entering into competition with each other for individual projects. Secondly, the element of risk to the contractor under such arrangements is very great indeed. Contractors already bear a heavy burden of risk under normal contracting procedures and this is especially so in developing countries. Indeed, the World Bank in its recent report on the construction industry in developing countries sees 'the central issue in the development of a country's construction industry as the growth of human capacity to manage these risks.'[17] The weakness of the local contracting industry in many countries means that there are not many local firms willing or able, to accept the additional responsibility and risk involved in organising design as well as the production process, and even if there were, the cost to the client would probably be high. Thus the widespread use of package deals would necessitate a continued dependence upon foreign contractors. This fact, together with the wastage of resources that the use of such a system entails means that its use in developing countries may well be restricted to very large contracts where internationally-owned consortia are invited to compete.

The conclusion seems likely that in developing countries there is no easy or obvious solution to the problem of re-structuring of the relationships between the various participants in the construction process in the private sector of the economy. It is therefore perhaps to the public sector that one should look for a closer integration of design and production, and for a more stable construction industry to emerge. For the public-sector is able, indeed as a major client it is obliged, to take a longer-term and more comprehensive view of the construction process as a whole. It is also in the public-sector that indigenous technical resources (at least in some of the poorest countries) tend to be concentrated.

It has already been noted that there exists in probably all countries in the world today some form of direct labour force. Direct labour (sometimes known as 'own account' or 'force account' construction) is the term that is used to describe a situation where the client (who may or may not be the actual future user or owner of the project) builds for himself with his own directly-employed labour force and his own directly-purchased or produced materials. It is a system that is frequently used by large clients of the construction industry, particularly public-sector clients, in market as well as planned economies. It is an especially suitable method for undertaking routine and preventive maintenance work, as this can be organised on the basis of a continuous programme. But it may also be used for new construction works so long as there is a fairly steady flow of work to keep the labour force (which is generally employed on a permanent, or at least a semi-permanent basis) fully-employed.

Direct labour organisations have in fact played an important role in the history of construction in Africa. They are most commonly found under a central government ministry of public works, which is often charged with the responsibility for the maintenance of all buildings and works in the public-sector. They may also be found in large local authorities, such as city councils, or even in universities and other types of parastatal organisation. In addition to a substantial core of supervisors, craftsmen and labourers they invariably have a team of architects, engineers and surveyors, directly employed on a salaried basis by the public-authority itself. Such an organisation, with designers and producers employed quite literally 'under the same roof', amounts in practice to a design and build organisation in the public sector. As such, it could offer all of the advantages of a package deal situation and more besides. For not only is the responsibility for design integrated with the responsibility for construction, as with the package deal, but the responsibility for maintenance is thrown in as well; and the roles of client and producer are merged. Thus, a direct labour organisation has been described as a 'state of affairs that allows a project to be conceived, designed, constructed, and maintained under the overall direction and control of a single person ...

there can be no more salutory experience for an engineer than to undergo the chastisement of constructing the work that he has designed, and maintaining it thereafter'.[18] Moreover, the advantages to be gained from the integration of design and production under a direct labour system are not confined to each individual project. So long as it is assured of a continuous flow of work within the public-sector, an accumulated fund of knowledge and experience can be built up by the construction team and used to secure an improved performance, on the part of both the designers and the producers, on each successive job. Thus there is a very real possibility that better designs, based upon a more appropriate and genuinely indigenous technology, may eventually emerge.

Direct labour organisations also have the potential to offer a number of other advantages. First, the fact that the client pays the actual costs involved in construction, rather than an estimated sum that is calculated to include the overheads and profits of an independent firm, means that it should always be a cheaper way of building, provided that it is executed reasonably efficiently. In situations where contractors' profits are exceptionally high (as is the case in many developing countries today) it should be much cheaper.[19] In addition, direct labour work involves much closer control by the client over his own construction operations and therefore affords him an opportunity to raise the standard of workmanship and control the quality of the finished product. Finally, the continuity of work and the relative permanence of the construction team that is associated with direct labour operations presents an opportunity to secure the 'decasualisation' of at least a section of the construction labour force - hence opening up the possibilities for expanded and improved training facilities and programmes, for improved safety and other conditions at work, and for an enormous advance in the productivity of labour.[20]

It must of course be recognised that a direct labour organisation can only be as effective as the management that is appointed to direct it; and its performance can only be judged by the objectives which it is in fact set. There is not generally any direct or automatic financial incentive for good performance in such a body, and no easy means of evaluating it. Also, direct labour operations are not really a suitable means for the construction of large, one-off projects. It may therefore be necessary for the state to set up in addition one or more semi-independent corporate bodies or parastatals, to be responsible for the design and the production of large, new, public-sector construction projects. The objectives of such design and construction parastatals must, however, be very carefully formulated in order that they may realise their long-term potential. Profits must not be the sole overriding criterion of success. They should *not* be expected to compete on each and every project with the private sector, thereby destroying the benefits of continuity of work and working relationships. And they *must* be assured of a continuous programme of work. Most important of all, extreme care must be taken in formulating the objectives for design, within a parastatal, in order that more rational and more economic designs may be developed by the government, for government to use on its own construction projects - and maybe eventual adoption by the private sector as well. In this way, the state in developing countries may in fact be able to 'use the public-sector as a channel and a spearhead for introducing desirable changes in the structure and attitudes of the construction industry at large.'[21]

Thus, it has been seen that governments do have the *means* at their disposal to secure a fundamental change in the structure of the construction industry. The interesting question is whether or not they have the *will*. For such a policy would undoubtedly come into conflict with a number of strong vested interests. For example, foreign-aid donors who promote their own country's products and designs, or insist on international competitive tendering and hence the use of foreign designers, contractors, construction services and technologies. The various construction professions who seek to perpetuate the status quo, so far as it consists of expensive construction products and techniques and a continued high demand for their services. And most important of all, the clients themselves (whether public or private, foreign or local, and including governments) who often choose sophisticated, capital-intensive, non-standard construction designs and techniques as a sign of 'progress'. Much will depend upon the nature of the state, and of the interests which it represents and seeks to defend - which takes us somewhat beyond the realms of the construction industry. Further light should be thrown on this issue by the case studies presented in Part two.

NOTES

1. In a recent study of the construction industry in a broad sample of developing countries, the government's share in construction output was found to be between 63 per cent and 90 per cent, see F. Moavenzadeh, 'The Role and Contribution of the Construction Industry in Socio-Economic Growth in Developing Countries', unpublished report prepared fo: UNCHS, 1980. For Government's role in Tanzania see E.J. Wells, Expansion of Public-Sector Construction in Tanzania (National Construction Council, Dar-Es-Salaam, 1984).

2. UNCHS, 'Review of the Role and Contribution of the Construction Industry in Human Settlements Programmes and National Economic and Social Development', Report of the Executive Director of UNCHS to the Fourth Session of the Commission on Human Settlements HS/C/4/3 (UNCHS, Nairobi, 1981).

3. F. Moavenzadeh, 'The Role and Contribution of the Construction Industry in Socio-Economic Growth in Developing Countries', unpublished report prepared for UNCHS, 1980.

4. Wells, Construction in Tanzania, p.5.

5. The argument is well summarised in P.P. Shrivastav, 'City for the Citizens, or Citizens for the City', Habitat International, Vol. 6 No. 1/2 (1982). For an account of the negative effects of site and service schemes upon the development of local building materials and construction industries, see L.R. Peattie, 'Some Second Thoughts on Sites and Services' and P. Siebolds and F. Steinberg, 'Tanzania: Sitesand Services', both in Habitat International, Vol. 6, No. 1/2 (1982).

6. G. Ofori, 'The Construction Industries of Developing Countries: The Applicability of Existing Theories and Strategies for their Improvement and Lessons for the Future: The Case of Ghana', unpublished Ph.D thesis, University of London, 1980.

7. See L.H. Muench, 'A Final Demand Approach to the Informal Sector and Implications for Public Policies' in 'The Urban Informal Sector in Kenya', Occasional Paper No. 25 (Institute for Development Studies, University of Nairobi, 1977).

8. Such as the support given by the Norwegian aid agency, NORAD, to the Tanzanian Building Research Unit for this purpose.

9. Corruption in Government dealings with the construction industry is both widespread and widely recognised. In some countries it has become institutionalised, e.g. in Nigeria, where a certain

percentage is allocated in tenders for this purpose.

10. The World Bank, for example, pays tribute to the role of direct labour organisations in the public-sector as a training ground for the (private) construction industry, but maintains that this is inevitably a less efficient - hence more expensive - method of construction, see World Bank, The Construction Industry: Issues and Strategies in Developing Countries (IBRD/World Bank, Washington, 1984). Evidence can in fact be produced to show the opposite, see Wells, Construction in Tanzania.

11. See for example National Board for Prices and Incomes, Report on Architectural Costs and Fees, Cmnd. 3653 (HMSO, London, 1968). For an appreciation of the problem in Kenya, see M. Wheeler 'Professional Fees of Design Consultants in the Kenya Building Industry', East Africa Economic Review (December 1969).

12. See for example H. Banwell, The Placing and Management of Contracts for Building and Civil-Engineering Works (HMSO, London, 1964).

13. For an interesting account of the development of the system of general contracting see G.A. Edmonds and D.W.J. Miles, Foundations for Change : Aspects of the Construction Industry in Developing Countries (Intermediate Technology Publications, 1984).

14. This proposal was put by David Burgess in an unpublished study for the Ministry of Economic Affairs and Developing Planning in Tanzania, see D. Burgess, 'A Study of the Construction Industry in Tanzania', report prepared for the Ministry of Economic Affairs and Developing Planning, Dar-Es-Salaam, 1970.

15. Graham Ive, 'The Role of the Public Client in Building Production', Proceedings of the Bartlett Summer School (Bartlett School of Architecture and Planning, University College, London, 1980).

16. See for example I.L. Freeman, 'Comparative Studies of the Construction Industries in Great Britain and North America: A Review', BRE Current Current Paper CP 5/81 (Building Research Establishment, Watford, Herts, 1981).

17. World Bank, The Construction Industry

18. S. Maynard Lovell, 'The Advantages of Direct Labour', Building (May 1969).

19. This seemed to be the situation in Tanzania in late 1983; instances were found where direct labour operations were as much as 60 per cent cheaper than construction by contractors, see Wells, Construction in Tanzania.

20. For the history of, and benefits to be derived from, direct labour operations in the U.K. See Direct Labour Collective, Building with Direct Labour (Housing Workshop of the Conference of Socialist Economists, London, 1978).

21. UNIDO, 'Construction Industry', Monographs on Industrial Development No. 2 (United Nations, New York, 1969).

PART TWO

CASE STUDIES

Chapter Six

KENYA: AN EXPERIMENT IN AFRICANISATION

BACKGROUND TO AFRICANISATION

Some of the difficulties confronting the construction industry in Kenya at the time of Independence have already been outlined in Chapter three. There was for example a very severe shortage of all kinds and levels of skilled labour; and yet no obvious or easy means of training. There were also serious bottlenecks in the supply of a number of essential building materials produced in Kenya and a lack of forward planning in the wholesale and distribution sectors. These shortcomings in the factor markets were aggravated by the adoption of inappropriate designs and the failure to adapt the technologies employed to the level of resources that was available. Consequently, prices were rising rapidly and there was a noticeable fall in the quality of work; trends which, in the absence of corrective policies, seemed likely to continue.

Overriding all of these problems in the governments' eyes, however, was the fact that the industry was completely dominated by firms owned and operated by non-citizens of Kenya - mostly of Asian origin. This situation had its origins way back in Kenya's colonial history when, immediately following the annexation of the territory by the British in 1895, the colonial authorities ordered the construction of a railway to run from Mombasa on the coast to Kisumu on Lake Victoria. Passing through the most fertile and productive parts of the colony, the railway was to open up the land to European settlers who subsequently established modern farming communities in the highland areas of the south-west of the country, the 'White Highlands' as they came to be called. The railway was actually built by contract labour brought over from the Indian subcontinent by the British specifically for this purpose. Many of these Indian (later known as Asian) contract labourers stayed on in Kenya after their contracts had expired. They began to accumulate capital in trade, transport and distribution; and a number of them moved into the construction sector.

Construction activity in the colony of Kenya expanded rapidly in response to European settler demands, as well as to the needs of the Asian traders themselves, and those of the colonial administration. The construction industry that developed followed closely upon the British model. Not only was it strictly hierarchical, but it was also clearly stratified along racial lines. Thus, the professional posts at the top of the hierarchy (architects and engineers) were occupied almost entirely by Europeans. There also developed a number of European contracting firms, operating mostly in the civil-engineering field. The vast majority of contracting firms however, as well as all of the middle-level posts in the industry, were the almost exclusive preserve of the Asian community. Similarly in the building materials industries a few of the larger firms producing materials for a national or regional market were owned by European capital - either foreign or domestic. But the great bulk of small and medium-sized firms, producing largely for local markets - and including the whole of the quarrying industry - were owned by Asians; as also was the distribution (importation, wholesale and retail) network. It was no exaggeration to say that the Asian community formed the backbone of the construction industry. Africans filled only the lowest positions in the hierarchy, unskilled and semi-skilled labourers and tradesmen. There was no more than a handful of very small African-owned firms.

Domination by the Asian community was not of course a situation peculiar to construction. Other sectors, notably trade and transport, were similarly dominated and subject to similar uncertainties as a result. Indeed, immediately following Independence Kenya's leaders made no secret of the fact that they intended to place high priority on (1) the encouragement of African commercial farming, replacing Europeans, under the various 'settlement schemes'; (2) the replacement of non-Africans by Africans in public-sector jobs; and (3) upon the 'Kenyanisation' of the commercial and service sectors. Consequently there was a great deal of uncertainty among the settler community as a whole, as to whether or not they would be allowed to continue to live and work in Kenya. The Asians, filling the middle levels of the economic hierarchy, had particular cause to be alarmed. The fact that the majority of them had failed to take out Kenyan citizenship after Independence was a reflection of this alarm. But it also aggravated the situation, for it seemed to indicate that they did not see their long-term future as lying in Kenya. Furthermore, with very few citizens of Asian origin, 'Kenyanisation' became, in practice, synonymous with 'Africanisation'.

It is important to understand that the motivation behind Africanisation proposals was essentially political. There was really no economic justification for the move. In the construction sector, there was no shortage of contracting firms and a healthy degree of competition existed between them. Asian-owned companies in transport, wholesaling, retailing, as well as in contracting were generally highly efficient organisations, operated on a very tight budget with extremely low overheads and a consequent high degree of flexibility. Some of these firms had already begun to move into industrial production. Thus, the Asian community, at the time of Independence, was already showing signs of developing into an entrepreneurial middle-class, or 'national bourgeoisie', and as such clearly had the potential to play a key role in the development process.[1] Many people saw this at the time, and there were consequently a number of exhortations to the Kenyan Government to slow down the move towards Africanisation, to give assurances to the Asian community regarding their political and economic future in the country and, above all, to ensure that those Asians who had taken out Kenya citizenship were not discriminated against - that what took place was Kenyanisation and not Africanisation.[2] Most of these pleas were in vain. The early leaders of independent Kenya had many demands on the part of the newly-enfranchised African majority to satisfy. Furthermore, it was in the interests of those in power to attempt to preserve the structure of the colonial economy intact. In order to meet these objectives they had quickly to create opportunities for an increasing number of Africans to attain a greater stake in economic life. The Asian community provided an easy scapegoat. Thus, from Independence on, African capital was encouraged to move into trade, transport, tourism, construction and eventually also into manufacturing industry to complement, or in many cases to replace, Asian capital. In this process it was strongly assisted by the state.[3] The successes, failures and effects of the process in one sector, construction, will be examined in this chapter.

THE NATIONAL CONSTRUCTION CORPORATION

Government's plans for Africanisation of the construction industry were announced in the First Five-Year Development Plan, 1965-1969.[4] Even before this time the Ministry of Works, which is responsible for the administration of all central government building, and a number of civil-engineering projects, had begun to reserve very small contracts exclusively for African-owned construction firms. And for larger contracts, a bias clause was introduced in the form of a tender price advantage in favour of African firms, so long as they agreed to reduce their price to that of the lowest bidder.[5] There were already some 200 of such firms registered by 1967. Some existed in no more than name; but a few were actively engaged in the construction of very small and simple buildings, or working as labour-only contractors to the Ministry of Works in gravelling roads. These small firms faced a number of difficulties, however. Even if they had some technical background, the majority had little experience of site organisation and little or no knowledge of managerial, commercial or administrative matters. They did not know how to tender for construction contracts. The plant and equipment they had was totally inadequate. And they suffered from a serious lack of capital. In addition, the suppliers of building materials and equipment (hardware dealers, or builders merchants, as well as all quarry owners) were Asians, not entirely sympathetic to the entry of Africans into the industry, and generally unwilling for this as well as for other reasons, to afford them credit. For all of these reasons, the preference afforded to African firms by the Ministry of Works proved to be an insufficient incentive, on its own, to enable African contractors to establish themselves in this very competitive market. Further and more direct assistance was clearly required. It was widely felt, however, that the Ministry of Works should not itself give such assistance, as its impartiality as administrator of a large number of government building contracts might thereby be jeopardised, or at least called into question. A quite separate body was therefore created as the government's chosen instrument for assisting African contractors to enter the construction industry. Known initially as the 'National Construction

Company', the name was changed shortly after its creation to the 'National Construction Corporation'.

The National Construction Corporation, or the NCC, came into being in the middle of 1967 as a wholly government-owned enterprise directly responsible to the Ministry of Works. Shortly after its inception a technical cooperation agreement was signed between the Kenyan Government and the Government of Norway, through its agency for international development, NORAD. Under this agreement a major Norwegian contracting company was commissioned to provide key personnel to the NCC and to act as a 'project counsellor' for an initial period of five years - which was later extended for a further five years. Some 13 specialist advisors, mainly for the building trade, were seconded by NORAD to the NCC; and each of these was assigned a Kenyan counterpart, seconded initially from the Ministry of Works.

The sole objective of the NCC was to assist African contractors to enter the construction industry. Despite its, perhaps misleading, title it was not originally intended that it should itself enter directly into production; but rather that it should help African firms to obtain work by acting as an intermediary between them and the government, as client; and subsequently to carry out the work through the provision of extension services, consisting of credit, advice and training. The NCC expanded rapidly after its inception, however, and during the process of expansion it changed considerably over the years. In 1972 it was transformed into a parastatal organisation and given considerably wider powers. The objective was still to 'promote and assist and develop the (African) construction industry'; but the new parastal was also specifically permitted to engage directly in production in the construction industry, as well as to 'do all such things, and enter into all such transactions, as it considers necessary for, or conducive or incidental to, the performance of its functions under the Act'.[6] Taking advantage of these new powers, the NCC began to expand in new directions - not all of them successful. For example, in 1975 an 'International Construction Company' was established to undertake contracts directly within Kenya, on a commercial basis. Sixty per cent of the shares were owned by the NCC and the other 40 per cent by a Yugoslav company, who also undertook responsibility for management under the terms of a management agreement. The company appears to have undertaken a couple of contracts before it got into serious difficulties, allegedly due to the high salaries paid to the large number of expatriate (Yugoslav) staff. In 1978, while undertaking construction of the new Kenyatta hospital, it was forced to stop trading, with accumulated liabilities of some nine million shillings. The expatriate managers left the country, the debt was taken over by the Ministry of Works and an Asian firm was called in to complete the work on the hospital. This particular experiment was never repeated.

Other difficulties arose from the fact that although the NCC as a parastatal organisation clearly had a great deal of autonomy, it was not expected to be self-financing. Thus, although it did generate some income internally (from rents on property owned, hire charges for plant and equipment, and interest and service charges levied from contractors) this income was used to augment its own revolving loan fund, rather than to cover its overhead costs. All recurrent costs of the Corporation were in fact paid by the Treasury, through its annual subventions to the Ministry of Works. As might perhaps have been predicted in this situation, there was nothing to check the growth of recurrent costs - which increased significantly over the years from a modest 0.17 billion shillings in 1967/78, to 5.3 billion in 1977/78 (when Norwegian assistance came to an end), to 14.6 billion in 1981/82. During the same period, the number of Kenyan staff rose from 15 to 246. While it is true that the volume of contracts handled by the NCC also increased, the proportionate increase in 'turnover' was far less than of either staff or recurrent expenditure.[7] Not surprisingly, the NCC - along with other parastatals - was eventually severely rebuked for its lack of financial discipline. Thus, in his budget speech for 1981/82, the Minister of Finance noted that 'the management of some parastatals remains ineffective; public accountability is often lacking and (there is) an over-dependence on the Treasury ... even where operations are potentially viable'. He announced the 'imposition of strict financial discipline within the parastatals'.[8] These statements were understood not to place in question the continuation of government grants to cover NCC operating expenses. But they certainly did not auger well for any expansion of government spending on the Corporation. And it was quite clear that the NCC was under serious pressure to improve its overall performance.

A new General Manager was appointed to the NCC in 1983. In an interview with the author in December of that year, he expressed his intention of enhancing NCC's record of contracts successfully completed by forcing NCC contractors to compete for subcontracts. He also intended to generate more revenue for the NCC by making sure that all loans were recovered and by charging for the services rendered to contractors. An increase in interest rates to a commercial level was also being considered. Despite these excellent intentions, however, the NCC remained insolvent. Its 'local purchase orders' were not being honoured and at the time of writing it is described as being 'at the point of collapse'.[9] For this reason, as well as the fact that it is the past achievements and reverses that are being examined and evaluated, in what follows the NCC will be referred to in the past tense.

WHAT DID THE NCC ACHIEVE?

From the beginning, the basic philosophy of the NCC was that of 'learning by doing'. The idea was that African contractors would be assisted and trained during the process of actually carrying out construction projects. But in order to carry out 'on-the-job' training, there were two other prerequisites; contractors had first to obtain work and then to obtain the finance required to complete it. Thus, the NCC had three functions: (1) helping contractors to obtain work; (2) providing them with adequate finance; and (3) assisting them in the actual process of construction. According to a former (Norwegian) General Manager, the Corporation was in fact conceived of as a combination of a school, a bank and a construction unit.[10] Despite the changes that took place over the years this three-pronged approach was never really challenged. Each of the three aspects - training, finance and the provision of jobs - will therefore be examined and assessed in turn.

The NCC as a 'School'

In the early years of the NCC the field staff consisted of 13 building supervisors. Initially all Norwegian, but with Kenyan counterparts, they were allocated to the various provincial offices of the NCC and each assigned a number of contractors to assist. The exact type of assistance rendered would obviously vary, in practice, with the ability of the contractors and the circumstances of the particular contracts on which they were working. But, according to the Corporation's first general manager, it was supposed to cover any, or all, of the following services:[11]

1. The building supervisor would accompany the contractor when the site was first handed over - in order to ensure that all contractual formalities were taken care of, the contract documents understood, and practical procedures for site inspections, variation orders, interim certificates etc. agreed upon.
2. He would help the contractor to work out a site layout and organisation plan and assist if necessary with the setting out of the building.
3. He would advise the contractor on the procurement of equipment and materials and help him to deal with suppliers and contors.
4. He would help the contractor to prepare a progress chart, to plan manpower and other resources and to follow-up the progress against the plans.
5. He would discuss with the contractor the financing of the contract and help him to prepare a loan application.
6. He would assist in book-keeping, cost-recording, keeping site diaries and all other paper work.
7. He would assist and instruct in general supervision, quality control, coordination and site safety.
8. Finally, he would guide the contractor through all phases of final inspection, handing over, final measuring and payment, maintenance period obligations and release of retained money.

The idea was that a building supervisor would in this way help each of his contractors through several jobs, closely monitoring their performance and progress and eventually leaving them to operate on their own. Throughout its history, this kind of informal, on-the-job training was an integral part of the activities of the NCC.

A fundamental contradiction in this approach quickly emerged, however. For the training to be effective, it was obvious that the number of contractors allocated to each building supervisor must be strictly limited. In fact, a maximum figure of 5 to 6 was arrived at on the basis of the assumption that at least one day per week should be spent with each firm. But this in turn meant that only very few contractors could be helped - only a tiny percentage of those who had come forward for registration. The weakness, in practice, of procedures for the 'graduation' of contractors no longer requiring assistance from the NCC further added to the difficulty. Thus, in an attempt to reach in its training efforts a much larger number of potential African contractors, as well as to further upgrade the general abilities of the contractors already receiving help, NCC management decided, in the early years, to arrange some formal training courses as an adjunct to its advisory service.

At first, formal training was performed part-time by two members of the NORAD technical assistance team, the senior building surveyor and the chief accountant. They visited each of the provincial offices of the NCC, giving six short training courses in 1968/69, and a further ten in 1969/70, to a total of 315 participants. As a result of these initial experiments, NCC management decided that there was an enormous unfulfilled need for formal training, especially in basic book-keeping, in understanding drawings and specifications, in planning, in estimating and in tendering; and that it should therefore become a full-time occupation for specialists. In 1970 a formal education section was established in the NCC, with an additional full-time engineer and an economist/accountant. During the first year of its operation some twenty courses, each lasting from three to five days, were given for 363 participants. In addition, the trainers were available to consult, on an individual basis, outside of lecturing hours.

It appears, however, that the contractors (or aspiring contractors) attending the courses were not so convinced of the necessity of proper training. Thus 'few contractors felt their major problem was learning how to run a complex construction organisation; many seemed to feel that if the government provided contracts and finance, the business would take care of itself'. And 'too many contractors considered a week's course an entry into business.'[12] Over the years it proved more and more difficult to maintain the level of participation in these formal training sessions. The number of courses offered was gradually reduced, the training specialists were not retained and the responsibility for training was handed back to the building supervisors in the NORAD team. After 1970/71, formal training never again figured prominently in NCC activities.

Informal, on-the-job, training did continue. In fact the majority of NCC specialists were engaged in what may broadly be called an 'advisory service'. Over the years a further contradiction emerged however in the form of a potential conflict between the dictates of production and those of training. This became more and more real as the NCC began to take on more direct responsibility for the actual completion of projects. In an attempt to re-emphasise the importance of training, the title of building supervisor was changed to that of 'building instructor'. But despite the change of name, they in fact became increasingly preoccupied with the actual supervision of contracts, rather than with the training in supervision of their contractors. Thus training, whether formal or informal, gradually became less central to NCC operations. Attention instead came to be focused on other aspects of its work - the provision of finance and the acquisition of contracts.

NCC's Role in the Provision of Finance

During the first few months of its operations the NCC did not make loans itself, but acted as a 'guarantor' for loans issued to contractors by the Industrial and Commercial Development Corporation - a body established to assist small Kenyan business in general. Loans were given in cash. No procedures were developed to collect the outstanding debts. And there was no strong incentive for the creditor to legally enforce payment because he was in any case covered by the guarantee from the NCC. Consequently a large part of these early loans were never recovered.

In 1968, NCC's own revolving loan fund was set up with a two million shilling grant from the Kenyan Government. The following year a further two million shillings was added by NORAD. Over the years the fund increased at a steady rate, augmented by periodic government grants and by the NCC's own internally-generated revenue. By 1981/82 eight million shillings had been added from the government and 20 million from NORAD; the fund stood at 30 million shillings.

Two types of financial assistance were offered to contractors by the NCC. Firstly there was direct access to cash in the form of working-capital loans for specific contracts. No more than 25 per cent of the contract value could be borrowed and interest was charged at 8 per cent (later increased to 10 per cent) on the outstanding monthly balances. Secondly, the NCC provided financial assistance to contractors through the issuing of 'performance bonds' at a flat charge of 3 per cent of the value of the bond, to be recovered over the first three interim payments.[13] As well as the provision of these types of direct financial assistance, the NCC in its early years was also instrumental in securing substantial indirect assistance to African contractors, by bringing pressure to bear on the Ministry of Works to relax a number of its contractual requirements. Among the more notable achievements was the decision by the Ministry to in fact waive performance bonds for all contracts up to a certain value if the work was to be carried out by African firms, as well as for some contracts in excess of that value at the discretion of the client. The NCC was also able to secure a reduction of 'retention money' (the maximum amount that may be retained by the client during the course of a contract) from ten per cent, to five per cent, and to 2½ per cent during the 'defects liability period', on Ministry of Works contracts. The net effect of all such concessions was that additional sums of money were made available by the client for use by the contractor - whose *need* for working capital was consequently reduced.

During the first few years of operation of the NCC's revolving fund, few processes for the 'screening' of contractors had been initiated. The available money was allocated very much on the basis of first come, first served. The 25 per cent limit on loans, compared with contract value, was not rigidly applied. Recovery systems were poor and some half of the money loaned was still outstanding at the end of the first year. Contractors who defaulted presented a dilemma. Should the NCC accept that they were 'failures' and simply write them off; or should they go on offering them financial assistance, in the hope that performance would eventually be improved and debts repaid? The NCC, in practice, tended to veer towards the latter course, and was subjected to a great deal of criticism as a result.

Gradually, however, enormous improvements were made in screening and administrative procedures.

Policy guidlines for loans were laid down by the Minister for Works, hence shielding the NCC from excessive pressure from contractors. These made it obligatory that a potential borrower should clear all previous commitments before being considered for a new loan, that he sould provide adequate security and that all loans should be recovered during the duration of the contract. The achievement of these objectives was greatly facilitated by the institution of the practice whereby the client made all payment, not to the contractor, but directly to the NCC, who subsequently deducted the sums outstanding in accordance with the repayment conditions of the loan before releasing the balance to the contractor. In addition, loans for materials purchased were granted, not in cash, but in the form of a 'local purchase order' (LPO), which could then be exchanged for materials with a builders' merchant, or wholesale store. By these means, the actual amount of cash handled by the contractor, and hence the temptation and opportunity for absconding, was significantly reduced. The record of debt recovery over the years (shown in Table 6.1) bears testimony to the effectiveness of such measures.

Table 6.1: Record of NCC Loans, 1967-1978

Year	(i) No. of Contracts	(ii) Contract Value	(iii) Loans Issued	(iv) Loans Re-covered	(v) Loans Out-standing	(v) as a % of (iii)
1967/68	32	5.67	2.46	1.11	1.35	55
1968/69	47	4.18	1.67	1.06	0.61	36
1969/70	109	15.30	3.54	2.93	0.62	18
1970/71	93	14.75	4.10	3.44	0.66	16
1971/72	163	26.86	6.02	5.42	0.60	10
1972/73	69	19.57	3.51	3.12	0.39	11
1973/74	26	13.61	3.46	2.38	1.08	31
1974/75	29	5.43	3.42	2.67	0.76	22
1975/76	33	27.80	5.48	4.06	1.42	26
1976/77	46	59.96	8.48	6.48	2.00	24
1977/78	82	54.51	15.65	13.64	2.01	13

Units: millions of Kenyan shillings

Source: Derived from Relf, C. (1981).

From Table 6.1 the significant growth in NCC's financial operations during the first ten years of its existence can be clearly seen. Thus, while the *number* of contracts carried out by African contractors under the auspices of the NCC increased from 32 in 1967/68 to 82 in 1977/78, the *value* of such contracts increased almost ten-fold, from 5.67 to 54.5 million shillings. And the value of loans issued increased, over the same period, from 2.46 to 15.65 million shillings per annum. It should be noted, that these figures are in current prices; and there is every indication that inflation in the construction sector was quite significant during the period, perhaps in the order of 14 per cent per annum, at least from 1972 onwards.[14] But even after allowing for inflation, the value of loans issued clearly did, in real terms, increase quite substantially. And in spite of this increase in activity the percentage of debts outstanding at the end of each year declined steadily for a while and never again reached the level of the first two years. Furthermore, a large percentage of the debts outstanding at the end of any one year may not necessarily have been 'bad debts'. They may have been, and in many cases actually were, subsequently recovered. In fact, one authoritative source has estimated that of the total of 60 million shillings loaned by the NCC from 1967 to 1978, only three million shillings was found eventually to be uncollectable; this represents only five per cent of the loans issued, or 1.2 per cent of the total value of contracts undertaken.[15] NCC's record on loan recovery, at least up until 1978, would probably compare favourably with other institutions elsewhere providing credit for the establishment and operation of small businesses.

Recurrent costs of NCC operations did, however, grow rapidly over the years. Hence the total cost of the loan service, although impossible to estimate with any degree of accuracy, was probably high. In addition, NCC's record regarding the distribution of loans could perhaps be criticised. While 25 per cent of the contract value as the maximum for any one loan was in fact generally adhered to at the beginning of a contract, contractors were frequently able to negotiate increases if they subsequently encountered cash-flow difficulties. Thus, in practice, loans ranged from as little as eight per cent of the contract value, to as much as 70 per cent. Also, contract value itself varied widely and so therefore did the actual sums represented by these percentage figures. As a result, the value of loans received by the contractors was very unevenly distributed, with one contractor alone in 1978/79 acquiring 25 per cent of the total of loans issued and one half of the total loans being shared among just four firms.[16]

The uneven distribution of loans among NCC contractors, due to wide variations in the value of contracts, was clearly brought about at least in part by the absence of effective policies for the 'graduation' of NCC contractors from the protective framework it offered. Thus, although contractors were placed into categories according to the amount of assistance they required from the NCC, by 1981 the NCC had still not categorised any of its firms as being able to operate successfully totally without NCC help.[17] Consequently, even the few African contractors who had grown in their capacity to undertake work still turned to the NCC for financial assistance on large projects, for which their credit needs exceeded the security they could provide to commercial banks. In so doing they took a disproportionate amount of the sums available and effectively deprived a large number of smaller firms from receiving assistance from the revolving fund. There was no easy solution to this dilemma, of whether to assist a smaller number of large firms so that they may continue to grow, or a larger number of small firms. It was in fact something that plagued the NCC from the beginning - and may in large part be responsible for its eventual collapse. In 1983 the NCC was accused of having lent a very large amount of money to a very small number of people. Such accusations might have had less impact were it not for the fact that most of the beneficiaries belonged to the same tribe. But this familiar problem needs no elaboration here.

NCC's Role in Obtaining Work

It has already been noted that the Ministry of Works, even before the inception of the NCC, was demonstrating its willingness to help embryonic African-owned construction firms, by the effective reservation of all small building contracts for such firms and the operation on large contracts of a preference clause in their favour. These measures were not immediately successful, however, in securing a larger percentage of the market for African firms for the simple reason that many of them did not understand contract documents and did not even know how to prepare and submit a tender. One of the earliest tasks of the NCC was therefore to strengthen its own staff of quantity surveyors in order to assist African contracting firms in the preparation of tenders. Such an exercise was not without its contradictions. An NCC surveyor might well find himself simultaneously helping a number of firms to prepare bids, in competition for the same contract. The exercise of at least apparent impartiality in such a situation was obviously of paramount importance. But an even more serious problem with this approach was the high degree of competition for contracts that existed among aspiring African firms and the fact that the submission of tenders on an ad hoc, or 'one-off', basis, was unlikely to provide continuity of work for any of them. On the other hand, continuity of operations was essential, at least for selected contractors, if they were to successfully accumulate capital and grow into substantial and independent firms. The NCC therefore began the practice of itself negotiating directly with the Ministry of Works for contracts for simple, repetitive types of work (such as primary schools, or low-cost houses) suitable for execution by African contractors. The contracts were subsequently divided into various parts and sublet to individual subcontractors, a practice which continued throughout the history of the Corporation. In addition, from about 1977 onwards, the NCC began to use the wider powers it had acquired as a parastatal to submit tenders to the Ministry of Works, in competition with established private firms.

Whether obtained through negotiation or tender, it was never intended that building contracts awarded to the NCC would actually be carried out by the organisation itself; but rather that the contracts would be sub-let, either in their entirety or suitably broken-up, to NCC's African-owned firms. Nevertheless, as a result of these procedures the NCC inevitably began, albeit implicitly, to take on some of the responsibility for the actual delivery of public buildings, to the time and standards required. Consequently more staff were needed, particularly quantity surveyors and site supervisors, to manage NCC's subcontractors on larger products. The NCC began to charge between one and two per cent for these management services. On site the new responsibility was reflected in a subtle change in the role of technical assistance staff, who gradually came to resemble managers rather than advisors. Accusations were levelled at the Corporation that it was becoming 'production' as opposed to 'training' oriented.

A further step in this direction was taken with the creation within the NCC of a 'Task Force Unit' (TFU). The original objective of this unit was two-fold; firstly, to undertake small, urgent building tasks directly on behalf of clients; and secondly, to act as a 'rescue service' to complete contractual commitments where NCC contractors had failed or defaulted. In practice, most of the work of the TFU fell into the second category - the completion of projects for which the NCC had originally tendered. Its work expanded rapidly, in line with the operations of the Corporation and the apparently paradoxical increase in the incidence of contractor failure. By 1980, some 30 personnel were assigned full-time to the Unit.

Thus the NCC, over the course of its history, undertook increasingly greater degrees of responsibility, from assisting contractors to obtain work, to obtaining work for them, to actually executing contract work in its own right; a fact that would at least in part explain the continuous expansion of its recurrent costs. In order to be able to assess the extent to which these additions to the NCC's responsibilities and costs may have been justified, it is necessary to ask how successful was the NCC in its declared aim, that of providing continuity of work for its contractors?

It is in building, as opposed to civil-engineering, work that most small contractors start their operations - a fact which reflects the greater barriers to entry into civil-engineering, resulting from the greater scale of operations and greater use of plant and equipment. Thus, most of the progress made by African contracting firms, under the 'umbrella' of the NCC, was in the building section of the construction market. From the outset, the NCC focused almost exclusively on general building work of the least complex kind. Most of such projects in the public-sector in Kenya are the responsibility of the Ministry of Works, which consistently maintained its bias towards African contractors. No such bias existed in the private sector. The vast bulk of the work with which the NCC and its contractors were involved was therefore in the public-sector, for the Ministry of Works as client.

The success of African firms in obtaining, through the NCC, public-sector building contracts from the Ministry of Works can be seen from Table 6.2

Table 6.2: Analysis of Ministry of Works Building Contracts

	1978/79	1979/80	1980/81
(1) Number of contracts let to African firms:	102	178	103
(2) % of contracts let to African firms	66%	69%	61%
(3) Average value of contracts let to African firms: (K.shs. million)	1.05	1.02	1.18
(4) Average value of contracts let to Asian firms: (K.shs. million)	12.29	8.27	9.3
(5) % by value let to African firms:	18%	26%	18%

Source: derived from Relf, C. (1981).

It is clear from the table that the number of awards to African firms varied between 60 per cent and 70 per cent of the total, over the three year period. But contracts awarded to African firms were on average only one tenth of the size of those awarded to non-citizens, so that African firms actually undertook only 18 per cent to 26 per cent *by value* of all new Ministry of Works building work. Since building contracts let by the Ministry of Works probably represented no more than about 13 per cent of the total of Gross Fixed Capital Formation in construction in Kenya around 1980, it can be seen that African firms had actually captured only a very small percentage of the total market.[18] What is more, it was a declining percentage as public-sector building work in real terms began to fall, from about 1980 onwards.

In order to compensate for the fall in building work after 1980, the NCC made a determined effort to capture for African contractors a share of the still relatively buoyant civil works sector. A separate civil-engineering division of the NCC was created. This division was split into two sections, one for water supply and one for roads. In the roads division a few contracts for gravel roads were started, with a single contractor typically undertaking a subcontract for a five to ten kilometre stretch of a larger NCC contract. Greater success was achieved in the water supply field where, following a decision by the Ministry of Water Development to reserve projects of up to 50 million shillings for competition exclusively among African firms, a contract for 15 million shillings was awarded to the NCC and subsequently divided among 10 African subcontractors. In addition, there was felt to be considerable scope for NCC firms to undertake small rural dams, for which few large contractors were willing to tender.

One difficulty in the way of expansion into the civil-engineering field, however, was the availability of finance. Individual projects tended to be much larger in civil-engineering than in building and therefore placed much greater demands upon NCC's revolving fund. A closely related and even more intractible problem was that of the availability of equipment, the demand for which is very much greater in civil-engineering than in building, even when methods of construction are supposedly 'labour-based'. NCC did in fact establish a plant pool at quite an early stage of its life, from which items of equipment could be hired out to individual contractors who could not afford to buy them. But this was expanded only very cautiously; in 1980 it comprised only 38 items - including six trucks, two motor-graders, six concrete mixers, two dump trucks and a variety of minor items. It was therefore neither large enough, nor sufficiently well-stocked, to cope with the demands of civil-engineering work. Whether and how the pool might be expanded further was a difficult question to answer, given the large amounts of capital such action would require, the general shortage of capital funds and the need for the NCC to continue to assist contracting firms operating in the declining building section of the market.

Thus, with only very limited success in the civil-engineering, or public-works, section of the construction market, the NCC has in practice had to rely upon building contracts to keep its contractors in work. Quite apart from the low value of these contracts, the actual *number* of contracts awarded to African firms was not large (102 in 1978/79, 178 in 1979/80 and 103 in 1980/81). In relation to the total number of African contracting firms registered with the Ministry of Works (800 in 1972 and some 2,000 in 1983), or even in relation to the number of those officially recognised by the NCC, it was miniscule. Thus, the crucially important question arises as to how this strictly limited number of contracts was allocated among such a large number of competing firms?

The NCC has naturally always stressed that there should be fair and objective criteria for the selection of firms for NCC assistance. Some sort of evaluation system was worked out in the early years by the Norwegian technical assistance team. Whether, or how, this has been applied in practice over the years is very difficult to ascertain. It seems that there has never been any great difficulty for firms to register with the NCC; all who came forward and satisfied some pretty basic requirements were generally included on the register - albeit in category E.[19] These firms could not in practice expect to receive any help from the NCC in obtaining work. But if they could somehow obtain some experience on their own initiative, they may then apply to the NCC to be included in the next category D. This would increase their chance of being selected as possible subcontractors on projects for which the NCC submitted tenders. Once accepted as an NCC subcontractor, a firm was automatically eligible to take advantage of NCC's full range of extension services, including the various forms of financial and technical assistance. It should thereafter gradually progress through categories C and B, and finally into category A. The full range of categories into which NCC contractors were grouped, as well as the number in each group in 1979 and 1981, are shown in Table 6.3.

Table 6.3: Classification of African Contractors

Category	Number of Firms	
	1979	1981
Group A (self-sufficient)	0	0
Group B (needs occasional financial support)	5	6
Group C (requires financial support plus training)	26	50
Group D (requires the maximum of assistance)	48	143
Group E (recently applied for registration)	316	666
All Groups	395	865

Source: Vevstad, F. (1979) and Relf, C. (1981)

Thus, the key to success for African contractors with the NCC seems to have been their acceptance into Group D, and subsequent selection to join the favoured few who were assigned NCC contracts - and all of the subsequent benefits that followed. How firms have actually overcome this hurdle has not been publicised. Personal contacts and tribal background, according to rumour, have played a larger part than more objective criteria. While such rumours are perhaps only to be expected the element of truth in them seems to have led to the refusal of NORAD to continue its involvement after 1977.[20] The wisest course does not, however, lie in pursuing answers to questions about 'favouritism' in the application of procedures for both inclusion on the register and selection for particular jobs. A more important issue now is whether or not the achievements of some 15 years of NCC operation were sufficiently significant to dispel any general disquiet as to its methods and practical procedures?

THE NCC AND CONSTRUCTION INDUSTRY POLICIES: AN ASSESSMENT

On balance, the answer to the above question would appear to be 'no'. The most tangible achievement of the NCC is that, through the provision of loans and its active intervention as an intermediary in the tender market, it helped a small number of African contracting firms to capture a share of public-sector building work and a less significant share of civil-engineering work. On the other hand, African firms are still undertaking only the very smallest and least sophisticated of contracts. And their share of the total construction market is still miniscule. In order for them to capture a larger share of the market, as it is now constituted, they must be able to undertake larger and more sophisticated contracts and they must be able to compete in the market for these contracts with the established Asian-owned firms. Evidence suggests that by 1983 there were no more than a handful of firms with any chance whatsoever of achieving this. Thus, Africanisation of the contracting business, despite the efforts and costs of the NCC, still seems a long way away. Africanisation of the whole construction industry, from design through to the production of building materials and components, seems even more remote. In order to understand why this is so - why the policy of Africanisation has been pursued far less successfully in construction than in other sectors of the economy - we must return to a consideration of the problems confronting the construction sector as a whole.

It has already been noted that research into the construction industry in Kenya in 1967 showed the problem was *not* one of shortage of contracting firms. There were many such firms (mostly Asian-owned, but with some Europeans also) which were actively looking for work and, if allowed, were anxious to remain in Kenya. Indeed, Kenya was extremely fortunate, as compared with its neighbours, in having not only a small number of large contracting firms and a large number of very small firms, as is common elsewhere; but also a very substantial number of locally-owned, medium-sized firms, operating within its borders. These medium-sized, Asian-owned firms are extremely efficient, and have many advantages (such as ready access to materials, capital and additional supplies of (family) labour) not available to African firms. What is more, the number of Asian contractors in Kenya increased significantly during the 1970s, as many former traders and transporters, forced out of business by licensing laws and other legislation reserving such operations for exclusively African firms, found new outlets for their capital and business acumen in the construction sector.[21] By the 1980s the expansion in the number of contractors, together with the fall in the volume of new construction work, meant that competition for contracts among existing firms was extremely intense. Not only African, but also established European firms operating in Kenya were unable to find work. Thus, in strictly economic terms, Africanisation of the construction industry, as it was conceived - that is, the replacement of Asian by African-owned contracting organisations - made little sense. It was pursued for political rather than economic reasons.

The real problems confronting the construction sector in Kenya lay, not in contracting, but in the factor markets. There were severe shortages of skilled labour, inadequate supplies and high prices of locally-produced materials and components and a consequently heavy dependence on imported items, of both labour and materials. The situation clearly arose from a reluctance on the part of contractors, or others, to undertake long-term investment in the industry, whether it be investment in the training of local labour or for the local production of materials. Although it was frequently argued that this lack of investment resulted from political uncertainties, a more fundamental cause undoubtedly lay in the uncertainty of future work-loads, engendered by the prevalence of a highly competitive tendering system and a lack of control on the part of producers over product design. Thus, writing in 1973, a senior lecturer in engineering at the University of Nairobi found that the fragmented structure of the construction industry in Kenya, particularly the fact that there was separate legal responsibility for design and construction, resulted in a failure of construction capital to move into the production of building materials and components. Such a movement would in fact require a contractor with both design capacity and direct access to a market - such as did not exist in Kenya. Consequently, few component industries were established; and the few prefabricated building systems that were produced by interests outside of the construction industry, failed to develop because of lack of access to markets that were largely controlled by independent designers. The conclusion reached was that in Kenya there was no significant private construction sector with a capacity for innovation; consequently, a genuinely local technology, based upon locally-developed designs, failed to emerge.[22]

A similar conclusion was reached by the ILO in their investigation into alternative means for increasing productive employment in Kenya, in 1972.[23] The problems they perceived in the construction sector were highlighted as follows:

1. An overdependence on imported materials, components and machinery;
2. A critical shortage of management skills in medium and small firms;
3. Training that was both inadequate and inappropriate, being based largely upon imported objectives and curricula;
4. The persistent use of design and contractual procedures unsuited to the realities of the situation in Kenya;
5. Overspecification in design, with little attempt to research into new standards for performance and quality - existing, 'imported' standards being simply scaled down.

The ILO team also noted that the inadequacy of training was partly due to the conditions under which the industry was forced to operate - with uncertainty as to its future work-load, a lack of continuity of demand, delay in payments and insecurity in the supply of building materials. They felt that, under such circumstances, it was unrealistic to expect satisfactory training to be achieved within the industry. The training functions of public-sector building and construction bodies would therefore need to be considerably expanded. The ILO mission in fact proposed an action programme, whereby the public-sector of construction demand should be deliberately used as a part of a long-term strategy for: (1) the encouragement of local materials and components; (2) the development of new contractual procedures, adapted to the needs and abilities of African contractors; (3) the stabilisation of effective demand in areas where it is needed; and (4) training in supervisory and management skills. They also called for technological standards to be drastically revised, in order to bring them into line with local conditions and for the revision of both the content and the orientation of technical and professional training.

The Kenya Government partly acknowledged these recommendations for the expansion of supply in the factor markets. Thus, there have been continual calls in the five-year development plans for expanded local production of building materials and for the establishment of new industries ...'new enterprises will be encouraged to establish production capacities for these items (timber, ceramics, pipes, softboards, ironmongery, etc.), so as to reduce the monopolistic practices of the few enterprises that currently produce them.'[24] The requirements for training were also noted and a levy board was established to administer a training levy, at the suggestion of the industry. But in practice, government has contracted rather than expanded its own training activities and it has not itself invested directly in the production of building materials. Continuous price rises in both the building materials and the labour markets throughout the 1970s and 1980s would seem to reflect that monopoly and restrictive practices in materials production are by no means problems of the past.

Some lip-service was also paid to the need to control and standardise designs for construction projects, to increase labour intensity in the construction sector and to improve upon the planning and execution of government building and works programmes. But the only measures that the government has actually taken to achieve these objectives has been to set up a committee to examine the structure of professional fees, and a 'research and development' unit in the buildings department of the Ministry of Works. No action whatever materialised from the first of these measures; very little from the second. In practice, the opportunity for the Ministry of Works to impose uniform standards on building designs or practices was severely diminished, as control of funds for development projects was taken away from the Ministry in the late 1970s and handed over to individual client ministries; they were 'expected', but not obliged, to make use of the facilities of the Ministry of Works in project implementation. Subsequent moves to decentralise the design capacity of the Ministry of Works buildings division, first to the provinces and then to the districts, only served to further weaken any move towards the standardisation and simplification of project design; as also did the recruitment to the Ministry of increasing numbers of recently graduated Kenyan architects and engineers - each anxious to leave his mark, or monument, upon the construction scene.[25]

Thus the record of the Kenyan Government's approach to the broader problems confronting the construction industry is not remarkable. It has persistently ignored calls for an expansion of the public-sector role in training; for rationalisation of the building materials and components industries; for greater public-sector control over standards of construction design; and for the simplification and rationalisation of contractual procedures. At least in part as a result of this neglect, building costs rose from 1972 onwards, at an average rate of approximately 14 per cent per year - well above the general rate of inflation.[26] High prices and low productivity in the construction sector - as in other sectors of the Kenyan economy - are today the cause of considerable concern, and a major factor impeding the implementation of development plans and programmes, as well as the movement of the economy on to a higher and more productive plane.[27]

It is perhaps in the light of this record in the broader field of construction industry development that the policy of 'Africanisation' of the construction sector, and the NCC's progress in achieving this objective, should be considered. When viewed from this perspective, there can be little doubt that the achievements of the NCC fade into insignificance. After all, there can be no intrinsic value as such in developing an African presence in the contracting industry, unless African firms can be shown to be somehow more efficient, more labour-intensive, or more likely to invest in the development of productive resources, than their Asian counterparts. There is no evidence whatever to indicate that this may in fact be the case.[28] On the other hand, the difficulties encountered in nurturing a handful of firms to the point where they may reasonably be expected to stand on their own feet and compete on equal terms in the tender market, appear to be so significant that one must question whether the general contracting firm and the competitive tendering system (both of which are alien imports) are in fact the only, or the most efficient, means of developing a genuinely indigenous construction industry?[29] Maybe the considerable resources placed at the disposal of the NCC could have been better-directed - towards the achievement of a more rational structure for the construction industry? Maybe its objectives should have been more clearly defined? Perhaps a 'lost opportunity' is the most appropriate way in which to view the whole experiment?

NOTES

1. A point made by C. Leys in Underdevelopment in Kenya: The Political Economy of Neocolonialism, 1964-1971 (Heinemann, 1975).

2. See, for example, T. Aldington et. al., 'The Economics of Kenyanisation', East Africa Journal (March 1968).

3. For a detailed analysis of the process in the industrial sector see N. Swainson, The Development of Corporate Capitalism in Kenya: 1918-1971 (Heinemann, 1980).

4. The term 'Africanisation' is used throughout this chapter in preference to 'Kenyanisation', as there was never any pretence in the construction sector to offer state assistance to (or discriminate in favour of) firms owned by Kenyan citizens of Asian origin. Assistance and preference were clearly intended only for Africans - which is perhaps understandable in view of the vast superiority of Asian over African firms, in terms of technical knowledge, experience and access to resources.

5. For contracts up to 5 million shillings in value there was a bias of 5% in favour of African firms; from 5 million to 20 million shilling contracts, a bias of 2½%; and for contracts of from 20 to 50 million shillings, a bias of 1%.

6. Republic of Kenya, National Construction Corporation Act (Government Printer, Nairobi, 1972).

7. C. Relf, Helping Towards Self-Reliance: An Analysis of Government-Sponsored Assistance to Small-Scale Contracting Enterprises in Kenya, Swaziland and Botswana (International Labour Office, Geneva, 1981).

8. Hon. M. Kibaki, Budget Speech for 1981/82 quoted in Relf, Helping Towards Self-Reliance.

9. Opinion expressed by the chief quantity surveyor in the Ministry of Works and by a number of other individuals in both the public and private sector.

10. See F. Vevstad, 'NCC of Kenya: An Approach to the Development of an Indigenous Construction Industry', Construction Management Programme, Case no. 1 (International Labour Office, Geneva, 1979).

11. Ibid.

12. Ibid.

13. Performance bonds are required on most contracts to the value of 7½% of the contract sum in the public sector and 10% in the private sector

14. According to the Construction Cost Index published annually by the Government of Kenya, construction costs rose by 20% in 1973, 30% in 1974, 17% in 1975, 3% in 1976, 8% in 1977, 9% in 1978, 15% in 1979, 21% in 1980, 12% in 1981, 14% in 1982 and 5% in 1983 - an average of 14% per annum over the 11 year period; over the 6 year period, 1972 to 1978, the average annual cost increase was also 14% per annum.

15. Vevstad, 'NCC of Kenya'.

16. See Relf, Helping Towards Self-Reliance.

17. See Table 6.3. By 1983 a total of 7 firms were officially included in category A; but according to the chief quantity surveyor at the Ministry of Works, only 3 of these were still in business.

18. Total capital formation in construction was 310 million shillings in 1980, of which 84 million shillings was in public-sector building work; only approximately 50% of public-sector building work is actually executed by the Ministry of Works (the rest being parastatal or local government building) - which makes 42 million shilings worth - or approximately 13% of the total. See Republic of Kenya, Statistical Abstract (Government Printer, Nairobi, 1983).

19. See Table 6.3.

20. NORAD's position on this matter was set out in a letter to the author dated 9th March 1983.

21. K. King, The African Artisan: Education and the Informal Sector in Kenya (Heinemann, 1977).

22. See P. A. Campbell, 'Legal, Economic and Technical Problems in the Establishment of Construction Industries in Developing Countries, with particular reference to Kenya', Technical Meeting on The Construction Industry in Developing Countries, ID/WG.148/8 (UNIDO, Vienna, 1973).

23. See International Labour Office, Employment, Incomes and Equality: A Strategy for Increasing Productive Employment in Kenya (ILO, Geneva, 1972).

24. Republic of Kenya, Fourth Five-Year Development Plan, 1979-1983 (Government Printer, Nairobi, 1979.

25. This point was made by a former chief quantity surveyor in the Ministry of Works. It is also interesting to note that Kenya has the dubious distinction of the largest number of nationalities with design offices in the capital; in fact, Nairobi is regarded internationally as something of a bonanza for design consultants - as the number and variety of high-cost buildings erected in the capital in recent years bears witness to.

26. See Construction Cost Index, Statistical Abstract, 1984.

27. For an interesting and comprehensive analysis of the need for such a movement see G.N. Kitching, Class and Economic Change in Kenya: The Making of an African "Petite-Bourgeoisie, 1905-1970 (Yale University press, 1980).

28. The point is very well made by B. Balkenhol, 'Small Contractors: Untapped Potential of Economic Impediment? Some Observations on the Construction Industry in Cameroon, Niger and Sierra Leone', World Employment Programme Research Working Paper WEP 2-22/WP.48 (International Labour Office, Geneva, 1979).

29. Ibid.

Chapter Seven

TANZANIA: NATIONALISATION WITHOUT CHANGE

At the time of the achievement of political independence in the early 1960s the construction industry in Tanzania was essentially similar to that of Kenya. Thus, it was based upon the British model, essentially hierarchical, with a few European-owned firms (consultants and large contractors) at the top of the hierarchy. Asian-owned firms occupied the middle and lower levels of general contracting, subcontracting, quarrying, materials production and distribution, and trade. But although basically similar to the Kenyan industry, in a number of ways it was far less developed. There was very little local production of building materials and very few quarries outside of Dar-Es-Salaam; so that prices of quarry products at times reached quite exorbitant levels and in many parts of the country there was simply no alternative but for contractors to produce their own. Due to an almost complete absence of technical training in pre-independence days (in what was in fact a British mandated territory) there were no African firms at all in the contracting business, in fact no Africans in the industry above the level of general foreman. And largely as a result of the absence of a strong settler community, there was a very much smaller number of European and Asian-owned firms, most of them in building as opposed to civil-engineering and many of them simply branches of Kenyan-based firms. Consequently, a high degree of collusion was clearly apparent among contractors in the tender market; there was an almost complete absence of any sort of real competition. Shortages in the factor markets and inadequate capacity in contracting both contributed to high and rising prices for construction products, with the consequent threat of budgetary contraints on the implementation of development plans.

Even more serious than the development of budgetary or financial constraints, however, was the fact that in Tanzania there was on occasions an absolute shortage of construction resources, representing a physical constraint on the execution of construction projects. Major new construction projects (such as the construction in the 1960s of the University of Dar-Es-Salaam) might attract into the country substantial resources under the umbrella of foreign-owned construction firms. And contractors for small, relatively simple, building projects could generally be found among the locally-based firms. But for projects falling in between these two extremes (that is, medium-sized, relatively complex, or civil-engineering projects, or any projects in remote up-country districts) frequently no tenderers could be found at all. The situation deteriorated further in the 1970s when, following the passing of the Acquisition of Buildings Act, 1971, whereby all rented property above a certain value was effectively nationalised, a substantial number of skilled Asian personnel from the building industry departed for Kenya, or further afield. Thus, the most serious overriding problem confronting the government in Tanzania was that of inadequate capacity in the construction sector, due to a lack of development of local resources and almost complete absence of local (African) technical expertise.

'Africanisation' of the contracting industry, however, in the sense in which it was adopted as a policy in Kenya, was never seriously considered as a policy option in Tanzania in the 1960s - despite the fact that it might have made more sense in the Tanzanian context than in Kenya, where inadequate contracting capacity was *not* a major problem. It was not considered for two reasons. Firstly, because there were virtually no aspiring African contractors at that time, due to the grossly inadequate level of technical training in pre-independent Tanzania and the low level of entrepreneurial skills that existed in general. And secondly, because by the late 1960s Tanzania had set itself the task of achieving greater economic independence and development through a policy of 'socialism and self-reliance', under which individual initiative and entrepreneurship was looked upon with suspicion and private capital accumulation was not to be encouraged.[1] So that the possibility of providing state assistance for the development of a privately-owned construction industry was not on the agenda in Tanzania. Thus, the major role in the development of productive forces in the construction sector, as in all other major sectors of the economy, fell to the state. Unlike Kenya, government in Tanzania was to involve itself directly in production in the construction field.

PUBLIC-SECTOR INVOLVEMENT IN CONSTRUCTION IN TANZANIA: EARLY EXPERIENCE.

In common with all British colonial territories, Tanzania under the British mandate had a ministry of public works which was responsible for overseeing the implementation of all government construction programmes and for the repair and maintenance of all government-owned assets. The ministry had a small direct labour force. It played an important role in the provision of employment, and some training, for Africans in the construction industry - albeit only at the lower levels. But it did not have the resources required to undertake the construction of major new projects on its own.

The first post-independence steps towards a more active public-sector involvement in the construction industry were taken in 1964 with the establishment of the National Housing Corporation (NHC). The overriding objective of the NHC from its inception was quite simply to build houses, particularly low-cost houses. Initial experience was encouraging. Unlike the National Housing Corporation in Kenya, which was essentially an institution for channelling finance to private-sector builders, the NHC in Tanzania immediately set about building-up its own capacity for design and construction, as well as for the production of building materials. Its methods of operation were quite different from the system prevailing in the private sector. Projects were planned and designed by the NHC staff. Designs for houses were simple and standardised, many of them following the conventional six-roomed 'Swahili' layout common throughout the coastal regions of East Africa.[2] Materials and components were also standardised, centrally-produced in NHCs own workshops and factories and delivered to the housing sites by the NHC itself, or its subsidiary 'Tacona'. Teams of craftsmen and labourers were then employed directly by the Corporation to complete the houses on a 'piece-work' basis, trade by trade, supervised by the NHCs own building inspectors who were specifically trained for this purpose. The method of employment and organisation of resources was in fact essentially similar to that prevailing in Britain in the eighteenth century, or to that used by the early colonialists in East Africa, before the rise of the general contractor and the separation of the professions.[3] Proof of the greater rationality and effectiveness of this method of organisation of materials and skills may be found in the fact that the NHC was from the beginning almost entirely 'Africanised'; and that the costs of construction, at around 20 shillings per square foot of living space, were probably the lowest prevailing in East Africa at that time.[4]

A further attempt by the government to participate directly in construction was more problematic. In 1966 the industrial arm of the Tanzanian government, the National Development Corporation (NDC) took over a minority shareholding in a local building company 'TECCO'. TECCO was owned and operated by Tara Singh Dogra, an Asian who had been in the building business since the 1920s. The following year the NDC purchased Tara Singh's shares and became the sole owner of the company. The name was changed to 'Mwananchi (peoples') Engineering and Construction Company', or 'MECCO'. In 1967, in an attempt to expand the company to play an increasing role in the industry, the NDC sold 40 per cent of the shares for two million shillings to a Dutch construction company of international repute. Thus, 'Overseas Construction Company' (OCC), a member of the Nederhorst group, became the minority shareholder in MECCO. More capital was injected into the firm and a management agreement was signed - under which OCC was to provide technical and managerial expertise, to run the company efficiently, to keep its accounts up to date, to set up financial control systems on its building sites and to train Tanzanian craftsmen and technicians to eventually take over. In return for these services, OCC would be guaranteed an income of 100,000 shillings per annum, together with a management fee of one per cent of the turnover of the company.

At about the same time, with an increasing amount of public-sector construction work about to come on to the market, the NDC saw an opportunity for a further potentially profitable venture in the form of a parastatal design company, or consultancy. The 'National Property Development and Management Corporation ' (NPDMC) - whose name was later changed to the 'National Estates and Designing Company' (NEDCO)- was established, with the NDC holding 75 per cent of the shares and the minority of shares held by a German design firm, GBM of Munich. GBM also undertook to staff and run the company under the terms of another management agreement. The fortunes, or rather the misfortunes, of these two parastatal organisations were essentially similar - so only the story of MECCO will be told in some detail ...

By 1969, some two years after the takeover of shares and signing of a management agreement with OCC, MECCO was clearly in difficulty. It was making heavy losses on its construction work. The accounting system was confused and each site manager was using his own method of controlling costs. There was no effective training programme. But there were 20 expatriate staff in the company and the management was trying to bring in more. The situation might have continued like this for some time without government intervention, as NDC (effectively a parastatal holding company) was often willing to use profits from its efficient companies to cover losses made by companies such as MECCO. But in August 1969 the NDC was split up and its subsidiaries distributed among various ministries. MECCO became an independent parastatal under the Ministry of Lands, Housing and Urban Development - with no other organisation in a position to reduce, or cover-up, its rapidly-growing overdraft at the National Bank of Commerce.

Economy measures were taken in November of that year. The general manager and nine other expatriates were transferred from the company and five others brought in, reducing the expatriate team by five. And steps were taken to establish some kind of cost control. But government concern continued because while MECCO was still losing money, OCC was benefiting. In addition to the 100,000 shillings per annum, the one per cent of turnover management fee and the payment of expatriate salaries, there was evidence that goods were being imported from Holland that could have been purchased more cheaply elsewhere; that many imported items were 'over-invoiced'; that turnover (and hence the management fee) was deliberately being boosted by taking-on large contracts at a loss; and that OCC was actually using MECCO as a subcontractor on some of its own projects, at uneconomic rates, thereby transferring funds to the parent company and out of the country.[5]

It did not prove easy, however, for the government to remove OCC as managing agents of MECCO. An attempt to persuade them to leave voluntarily failed. The company was technically bankrupt; but when the

National Bank of Commerce threatened to foreclose if the overdraft was not repaid within a certain time, OCC appealed to the Dutch Ambassador and put substantial pressure upon Tanzanian leaders and officials, arguing that other foreign companies would lose confidence if the Tanzanian government acted like this. The Bank withdrew its deadline and pressed instead for financial and technical auditors to be appointed to examine the operations of the company. Finally, however, under pressure from MECCO workers concerned about employment practices and worker-management relationships in the company, the government stepped up its efforts to reach some sort of an agreement with OCC. In December 1970 it announced the purchase of OCC's minority shareholding and the termination of the management contract 'by mutual agreement' at the end of the year. The announcement stressed that no compensation would be paid to OCC. Nevertheless, by paying the company 2 million shillings for shares of negligible value, it appears that the government in fact paid them to leave.[6]

It took a further two years before the minority shareholding of the GBM in the NPDMC was taken over by the government and the management agreement terminated. Despite the difference in nationality of the minority shareholder and managing agent, and in the nature of the business, there were striking similarities between the two cases. The original agreement with GBM, like that with OCC, was extremely unfavourable to Tanzania. There was little attempt to run the company efficiently, or to train Tanzanians. And the parastatal was used to channel business to the parent company in Europe. So that while the Tanzanian subsidiary showed losses GBM, like OCC, managed to make quite substantial profits for themselves. The foreign partner seemed to lack integrity. The battle to terminate the agreement, made originally by the NDC with GBM, proved lengthy and vicious. But it did eventually succeed, and NPDMC was finally re-constituted as NEDCO, under 100 per cent government ownership, in 1972.

Thus, government involvement in the construction industry in the 1960s was mostly a negative experience. Apart from the limited initial success of the National Housing Corporation (which was in fact soon to be reversed)[7] it did not lay the basis for a solution of the major problems facing the industry; nor in fact was this broader objective uppermost in the minds of either the NDC or the government at the time when MECCO and NPDMC were established. The major objective in the establishment of the 'construction parastatals', as they came to be called, was quite simply to make money; or to obtain for government a share in the high profits being made in the private contracting industry. Other objectives also existed, or were later introduced, such as the expansion of capacity in the industry, increased efficiency, better training opportunities etc. But there was no attempt to evaluate the various objectives, and no possibility of conflict between them seemed to be considered. Rather it was assumed that if MECCO and NPDMC were to act as government-owned contracting and design organisations within the existing construction industry, then the profits would flow (to government) and all the other benefits besides.

It was also strongly felt at the time that in order for MECCO to be efficient - or, more precisely, in order to be seen to be efficient - then it must be obliged to compete for individual contracts with the private sector. But it is not easy for public-sector firms to compete with the private sector, and this is particularly true in construction (a point that was made at some length in Chapter five). Furthermore, it should have been questioned whether competition in the public-sector is in fact so desirable. For competitive tendering for construction projects, while conferring somewhat dubious advantages, has many serious disadvantages. It inhibits the stabilisation of the labour force and the provision of training; investment in the kind of machinery and equipment that even labour-intensive projects should use; and the development of resources on the part of the contractor. It therefore has very serious negative effects upon the level of investment and productivity in the industry as a whole. Government, in forcing its construction units to compete for each project, was forcing them to behave like the private sector and thus perpetuating a low-wage/low productivity spiral pattern at an unnecessarily low level. At the same time it was throwing away an opportunity to experiment with the potential advantages of public-sector units, to create a possibly more stable and productive kind of industry, based upon the principles of planning and cooperation rather than competition.

After the initial disappointing experience with MECCO, these points seem to have been understood, at least by some officials in the Tanzanian government. In late 1970, with the shell of a design company and the problem of a bankrupt construction company on its hands, the government commissioned a report on the future of the construction industry from an independent consultant. The terms of reference for the study were themselves instructive in showing how far government thinking had progressed. Thus, the consultant was asked to advise on the particular problems of establishing a parastatal construction capacity in the context of the general problems of the industry; and to assess how this could be done with maximum benefit to the industry as a whole. The task was seen as threefold: '(1) to form an opinion of the general problems of the industry; (2) against the background of the industry's situation, to advise on the problems of establishing a parastatal capacity that is soundly-based and has the capacity to expand relatively rapidly; and (3) to consider the extent to which this firm (or these firms) could play a role by virtue of their parastatal nature in improving the performance of the construction industry as a whole.'[8] Clearly much more was expected of the 'new' MECCO and NPDMC than the simple generation of profits.

The report that was duly presented to the government highlighted the basic inconsistencies in the structure of the construction industry in Tanzania and made the following recommendations:

(1) If the objective in the establishment of construction parastatals was simply to make profits for the state, then the two parastatals (one for construction and one for design) could continue to operate as before, in competition with existing private firms in the industry.

(2) If, however, other objectives were sought - such as the training of Tanzanians, expansion into the regions, and the production of more 'economic' building based upon standard plans - then the two parastatals must be able to plan a programme of work and the physical and financial resources required for it in advance. The current practice of competitive tendering for each individual contract should therefore be replaced by a system of negotiating contracts with government and other public-sector clients; negotiations should be on the basis of actual costs.

(3) Further, a number of these broader objectives could not be achieved if the parastatals were expected to 'maximise' profits

in the short-term; but rather a long-term perspective should be adopted and other objectives should be clearly spelled out, together with the means by which performance was to be assessed.

(4) Finally, the most important objective of the development of more rational designs, making more effective use of local materials and technical skills in short supply, could *not* be attained within the present structure of the industry but only under a system where architect and builder had equal authority, shared a common objective and were jointly responsible to the client for the final product. This could only happen if design and construction activities were integrated within a single body. MECCO and NPDMC should therefore be merged to form one single integrated 'design and construction' parastatal responsible for all stages of the construction process.[9]

Government reaction to these proposals was disappointing. Thus, while it was recognised in principle that there was a serious need for training and also for closer cooperation between architect and contractor in order to produce more economic construction designs, there was tremendous resistance to the idea of moving away from simple, profit-maximising objectives to a definition of broader social aims where performance may not be so easy to assess. And the fundamental proposal for integrating design and production within a single parastatal was very firmly rejected. Government instead reconstituted MECCO and NPDMC as quite separate entities, each operating in a traditional context, with managers recruited individually on the world market - later to be replaced by Tanzanians. In reality the overriding objective of the new companies was to make profits. And, despite the lip-service paid on occasions to the need to provide the parastatals with a guaranteed programme of work, in practice they were expected to obtain this for themselves in competition with private firms.

To the credit of the Tanzanian management of MECCO, they did in fact eventally succeed in fulfilling the government's aim; they were able eventually to generate profits for the state, operating in a contracting situation in competition with privately-owned firms. Thus, the government did succeed in establishing and maintaining one reasonably effective state construction company. It has, over the years, undertaken a number of important construction projects. At the same time it has served as a valuable training ground, in construction technology and management, for a number of young Tanzanians. Undoubtedly the construction industry in Tanzania would have been in a significantly worse state without it. On the other hand, the company has not had any great impact on the industry. With a maximum annual turnover to date of 150 million shillings, as against an estimated total construction demand in the monetary sector of the economy of 3.4 billion shillings in 1982, it can at best account for a tiny percentage of the total of new construction work.[10] Furthermore, operating not only on a limited scale but also in a purely conventional framework, it has clearly fallen far short of the original objective of securing a transformation of relations of production in the industry as a whole and the emergence of more economic structures through the adoption of more appropriate, rationalised and standardised designs. This point was quite forcefully put by a former (Tanzanian) general manager of MECCO. Writing in 1977, he argued as follows:

> More economic building will result from a careful section of materials, as well as by reducing actual construction costs. These benefits can be achieved if the contractors participate in the initial planning and design stage. It is very disappointing to note that ... the construction parastatals are not invited to participate at the design stage. MECCO has constructed the following buildings in Dar-Es-Salaam: NIC Investment House, Kariakoo Market, New Africa Hotel, Bank of Tanzania etc. ... these are all landmarks in our cities. The quality of these works is first class. MECCO has therefore acquired a fantastic wealth of experience in constructing all these structures. It is truly not in the interests of this country if this wealth of experience of our parastatals is allowed to waste .... The parastatal contractors should participate in final designs ... By bringing the parastatals into play during the design stage it also helps them to plan their equipment and manpower requirements well in advance.[11]

Despite such pleas, the experience of MECCO has indeed been allowed to go to waste, rather than being put to use in the development of more appropriate designs. And the parastatal has continued to be denied the advantages that would stem from the provision of a planned programme of continuous work.

The government did make other attempts, during the course of the years, to expand public-sector construction capacity - either through the creation or expansion of direct labour units for 'own account' construction; or through the establishment by Act of Parliament of 'corporate soles' for the execution of construction work under contract.[12] And it did, on occasions, appear to recognise the great benefits to be gained from the provision of stable employment in the construction sector and actually provide its construction units with guaranteed work. In fact, one construction unit under the Ministry of Works was established in Dodoma specifically for the purpose of providing ongoing employment for gangs of workers brought together for the construction of a major project (the TAZARA railway line) and in subsequent danger of being disbanded. So long as such units were supported, as the unit established in Dodoma was supported (at least initially) by the Party, they worked well. But the support eventually dried up. Left to compete for projects with the private sector, they could no longer guarantee work for their labour force and were forced to dispand.

Thus, the establishment of a state presence in the construction industry, while adding marginally to the capacity of the sector, has not resulted in any fundamental re-structuring of the relations of production within the industry; and it has not provided any real solution to the problem of the inadequate development of construction resources in Tanzania. Government has not been completely unaware of this situation; concern for the future development of the construction industry has in fact re-surfaced from time to time. On each occasion, a new report seems to have been commissioned. Following the recommendations of one of these, a 'National Construction Council' was established as a 'liaison and coordination body between ministries and parastatals concerned with construction'.[13] But the problems do not go away - as a glance at the state of the industry in the 1980s will clearly show.

CONSTRUCTION IN TANZANIA IN THE 1980s

By the beginning of the 1980s, it was quite clear that the Tanzanian government's stated objectives for the construction sector - a reduction in the import-content of construction programmes, increased capacity, improved efficiency, better design and increased public-sector participation - were very far indeed from being achieved.[14]

Construction activity in Tanzania in fact declined throughout most of the 1970s. From a peak level in 1973, when value-added in construction activity accounted for 5.3 per cent of GDP and gross construction output was 66 per cent of capital formation, output decreased in real terms each year until 1978, when it was only 3 per cent of GDP and 36 per cent of capital formation. Although this decline was in part due to the completion of a number of large civil-engineering projects started in the early 1970s, it also reflected the state of the economy in general and the lack of capacity in the construction sector. There was a short revival between 1978 and 1981 in the non-residential building sector, but output fell again in 1982 and 1983.

In 1982, capital formation in construction (a measure of gross output) was 4.3 billion shillings in current prices. Included in this figure was a sum of 0.7 billion shillings, being the estimated value of building in the subsistence sector, or 'own-account rural'. If this sum is deducted from the total, then the value of new construction work in the monetary economy was approximately 3.5 billion shillings. Two billion shillings of this was in civil-engineering work and 1.5 billion shillings in new building.[15]

The public-sector share of construction output is not identified in Tanzania. In the Ministry of Works <u>Local Construction Industry Study</u> (1975) it was estimated at 54 per cent of total construction, or 63 per cent of total construction in the monetary economy. An ILO report in 1983, however, estimated construction work in the public-sector to be 70 per cent of the total - and this sum excluded direct labour, or 'force account' construction.[16] In fact, data provided by the Central Statistical Bureau for 1980, 1981 and 1982, shows public-sector investment in construction to be consistently 80 per cent of total construction investment. As investment by the private sector is mostly in the subsistence, or non-monetary, sector of the economy, the public-sector share of investment in the monetary economy is even higher, at around 96 per cent; a total of 3.4 billion shillings in 1982. Of this total of 3.4 billion shillings, it is estimated that 460 million shillings of work, or 14 per cent of the total, may have been actually implemented by public-sector construction units.[17]

The rest of the public-sector construction programme - some 86 per cent or more of the total - was implemented by private-sector construction firms, either locally or foreign-owned. Unfortunately, the government has little control over the level of costs or prices, or over the general level of efficiency in the private building industry. With little or no competition operating between the small number of firms active in the market, both prices and profits are high. Consequently private firms have no incentive to increase their level of efficiency through investment in equipment or training of labour. Furthermore, it must be remembered that initial tender prices, even when high, are frequently well below the final sum paid for a project. In the sort of conditions prevalent in Tanzania, many opportunities exist to inflate the final contract sum and it may be assumed that such opportunities are fully exploited by contractors. Private consultants, supervising on behalf of public-sector clients, have nothing to lose and much to gain (at least in the short term) by allowing contractors' claims. Proof of the high level of prices and profits in the contracting market in Dar-Es-Salaam at the end of 1983 may be found in the fact that a number of public-sector clients were beginning to establish their own 'direct labour' teams, for implementation of new construction projects at from one-half to one-third of the cost of implementation by private-sector firms.[18]

In addition to the high degree of dependence upon the private contracting industry for the implementation of public-sector construction projects, Tanzania is also still very heavily dependent upon the use of foreign resources. The direct import-content of materials and equipment for a number of construction projects was found in 1980 to amount to over 50 per cent of total construction costs. There was also a very heavy dependence upon foreign firms and foreign personnel, from design right through to final execution. Although it is impossible to give an exact figure, the import-content, or total 'leakage' to the economy, may on some construction projects be as high as 75 per cent.[19]

The implications of this situation are clear. For since 1978 a series of factors have operated to weaken the Tanzanian economy. The second round of oil price increases (among other adverse trends in the terms of trade), a succession of bad harvests, and the Ugandan war caused serious shortages of foreign-exchange. When the situation deteriorated even further, restrictions on imported materials, components and equipment for both the construction sector and the local building materials industries, were imposed. Thus a supply of essential inputs to the construction industry is simply not available, at least, not at manageable prices. As a result there are delays, stoppages and unprecedented increases in building prices as contractors attempt to compensate for the additional costs incurred by the disruption of the work, the falling productivity of labour, unofficial 'black market' prices paid for materials and slow payment by public-sector clients - themselves suffering from problems of liquidity. The rate of inflation in the construction sector in 1984 was estimated to be as high as 50 per cent per annum. Cities abound with half-completed buildings, awaiting either the arrival of essential inputs or of additional funds. The construction industry in Tanzania in late 1985 was at the point of collapse.

Failure of the government to exercise any control over design was probably not helpful. This control could have been secured through the construction parastatals, MECCO and NEDCO. Decisions taken at the design stage of a project's implementation have the greatest impact upon the requirements for material inputs, the choice of techniques to be employed, the standards of construction that are to be met; they are therefore the most important single determinant of cost. And yet in the Tanzanian construction industry those responsible for design bear no responsibility for construction; they are not accountable, either to the client for the particular project or to the public at large, for the final results of their decisions.

The system under which power is allotted without responsibility cannot ever be said to have functioned effectively - even in Britain where it evolved.[20] But to function at all, such a system is dependent upon a number of factors:

(1) The presence of long-established and competent design consultants who are conversant with conditions in the industry and the country, and dependent upon their

reputation for continued assignments; this is especially important where the resources which comprise the construction industry are severely under-developed, as is the case in Tanzania;

(2) The presence of discriminating and technically experienced clients, who know what they want from their consultants and from the construction industry; and

(3) Some kind of ultimate accountability of clients to a wider public (such as exists between companies and their shareholders, or between council and their ratepayers, or governments and the people at large) so that they may be called to account for their use of public funds in construction projects.

Unfortunately, none of these exists in Tanzania. Although there are undoubtedly some competent and professional consultants, the majority are neither - as is evidenced by the fact that in 1983 and 1984 consultants were still accepting (in some cases actively soliciting) briefs for new projects which they knew could not possibly be built. And they were continuing to base their designs upon imported, hence non-available, products. This surely cannot be divorced from the fact that consultants are paid a percentage fee for their services, based upon the final cost of the project; and they are paid most of this fee before construction begins, and whether or not it begins.[21] To understand the effects of a dependence upon foreign private consultants for the execution of government construction programmes, one may do no better than quote again from the former general manager of the state construction company:

> In the absence of design control, the reliance on expatriate designers from different parts of the world results in the adoption of too many design standards. This has an adverse effect on the cost of projects, for quite often these designs tend to have disproportionately high import content in terms of materials, fixtures and equipment. The Tanzanian client, mostly the public-sector, suffers in four distinct ways ... first a costly design which results in relatively costlier building; secondly a high import content built in, which erodes further the already meagre foreign exchange of the country; thirdly he gets an inappropriate structure in terms of

> social and weather conditions; and fourthly he loses the opportunity of developing local talents and local materials ... The development of a local building materials industry could very well be stimulated at the design stage if the designers were sensitive enough to the country's economic, social and political situation.[22]

But it is not sufficient to blame unscrupulous, or uncaring, consultants for the shortcomings of the construction industry in Tanzania. The question remains as to how and why the Tanzanian government has allowed this situation to develop and to continue. After all, government has been a client of the construction industry for many years now. Why has it not learned to be discriminating? Why has it not learned to drive a hard bargain - to know what it wants from its consultants and insist that they deliver?

Even more important ... one may ask what has happened to 'public accountability' in Tanzania. In principle, all plans for new construction projects should be first approved by the Ministry of Planning. All subsequent commissions for design work should be channelled through the Ministry of Works, who are supposed to offer the projects first to the design parastatal (NEDCO) and only if they are fully-occupied, to the private sector. In addition, all proposals for the use of foreign-based consultants should be vetted by the 'Tanzanian Industrial Studies and Consulting Organisation' (TISCO). In fact, this voluntary system of control has never been fully implemented. And suggestions that it should be backed up by sanctions against offending parties - such as the Treasury refusing to release funds unless correct procedures have been followed - have not so far been taken up.[23] Worst offenders are the ever-increasing number of parastatal organisations, who have been allowed to use their own funds for development and have continued to commission designs for construction projects (mostly prestige offices in the cities and high-cost staff houses) directly from consultants in the private sector. In fact the growth in demand for new construction work on the part of these parastatals - whose share in total construction investment increased from 19 per cent in 1980 to 36 per cent in 1982 - has been a major factor responsible for the weakening of government control over the implementation of construction projects.

There is a further factor, however, that cannot be ignored. Parallel to its failure to control design and design standards, the Tanzanian government has allowed the continual run-down, over the years, of its major agency responsible for the implementation of such control. The Ministry of Works is in principle still charged with the responsibility for the execution of all public-sector construction programmes and for the subsequent maintenance of all government-owned buildings and works. It should do this either by undertaking the design and construction work itself (sometimes by 'direct labour'), or by supervising the implementation of such work by the parastatal or the private sector. However, continued depletion of the ministry's resources of trained and experienced manpower, together with its 'truncation' during the process of governmental decentralisation (with the severance of the link between the head office in Dar-Es-Salaam and district engineers responsible for the implementation of construction programmes in the regions), have rendered it increasingly incapable of performing its allotted tasks. At the same time, the proliferation of 'in-house' professional teams for the supervision of design, construction and maintenance work in a number of other ministries and in most of the parastatals has enabled them to effectively bypass the services previously supplied by the Ministry of Works, thus facilitating its further decline. With the running down of this major public-sector capacity for the supervision of construction work, government's ability to exercise effective control over standards of design or production in the industry has been inevitably reduced.

If the government of Tanzania wishes now to reverse the appalling decline in its construction sector and all that this implies, it would seem that it has no option but to take steps to regain control over the standards of its own construction projects and programmes; and this means control at the inception of a project, at the 'briefing' or 'predesign' stage. In order to do this effectively, it must start to re-build its *capacity* to control through re-developing its agencies for implementation chief of which is the Ministry of Works. Present levels of construction output, both in absolute terms and in relation to GDP, are extremely low by international standards, as well as in relation to what they have been in the past in Tanzania.[24] In the longer term there must therefore be a big increase in construction output if the economy is to develop. And in view of the severe and persistent foreign-exchange problems, it seems that growth will have to be based to a very large extent upon the development of local resources and simple techniques. The gravity of the situation, and the widening gap between aspirations and realities in Tanzania, makes it imperative that the government takes action now along these lines. Whether or not it has the 'political will and commitment' to do so remains very much an open question.[25]

NOTES

1. See J.K. Nyerere, The Arusha Declaration (TANU, Dar-Es-Salaam, 1967).

2. There were no architects employed by the NHC at this time.

3. For a description of such methods of organisation of the construction process see G.A. Edmonds, and D.W.J. Miles. Foundations for Change: Aspects of the Construction Industry in Developing Countries (Intermediate Technology Publications, London, 1984).

4. See E.J. Wells, 'The Construction Industry in East Africa', Economic Research Bureau Paper no. 72.2 (University of Dar-Es-Salaam, 1972).

5. A detailed description of how this was done on a number of projects may be found in A. Coulson, Tanzania: A Political Economy (Clarendon Press, Oxford, 1982), Appendix 2.

6. See Coulson, Tanzania: A Political Economy for an account of the sequence of events as related in this paragraph.

7. From about 1970 the NHC began to employ the services of an architect. The six-roomed traditional house-style was increasingly replaced by 2/3 bed-roomed single detached houses, with a corresponding increase in unit costs. At the same time, it began to employ contractors, even on very small projects, which contributed further to the increase in costs. By 1979/80 only 100 dwellings a year were completed, compared with 1,000 ten years previously. See Ministry of Works, Local Construction Industry Study (Ministry of Works, Dar-Es-Salaam, 1977); and Swedish Ministry of Housing and Physical Planning, 'Swedish Assistance to Human Settlements in Tanzania - A Feasibility Study', 1982.

8. See D. Burgess, 'A Study of the Construction Industry in Tanzania', Ministry of Economic affairs and development Planning, Dar-Es-Salaam, 1971.

9. Ibid.

10. In 1982 MECCO actually undertook 80 million shillings of work, representing 2 per cent of the total of new public-sector construction.

11. See N. Lemunge, 'The Experience of Public Construction in Tanzania', paper presented to a seminar on the Tanzanian Construction Industry, Dar-Es-Salaam, 1977.

12. 'Corporate Soles' were established under the Ministry of Works, the National Service and the Prisons Department. Their legal status has never been clearly defined. They have been described as 'direct labour units with the unit engineer, or project manager, acting as a managing director bound by no specific financial regulations except his own professional ethics', see Lemunge, 'Public Construction in Tanzania'. In 1984 it was proposed that such units be integrated into an expanded direct labour structure under the Ministry of Works, see E.J. Wells, Expansion of Public-Sector Construction in Tanzania (National Construction Council, Dar-Es-Salaam, 1984).

13. See Ministry of Works, Local Construction Industry Study.

14. Ibid.

15. See United Republic of Tanzania, Economic Survey 1982 (Government Printer, Dar-Es-Salaam, 1982).

16. See ILO/DFK, draft report on an ILO mission to Tanzania to advise on contractor support, October 1983.

17. The figure of 460 million shillings is made up as follows: 100 m. shs. of work by public-sector contractors (mostly MECCO); 260 m. shs. by ministerial direct labour forces operating on their own account (mostly the Ministries of Works and Water); and 100 m. shs. of work by direct labour units operating as contractors (mostly the prisons and the national service).

18. See E.J. Wells, The Expansion of Public-Sector Construction in Tanzania (National Construction Council, Dar-Es-Salaam, 1984).

19. This conclusion was reached on the basis of information provided in Barker and Barton, 'The Construction Industry in Tanzania: The Current Situation - November 1880', Barker and Barton (Tanzania) Ltd., 1980.

20. See chapter four.

21. Tanzania was still paying official scale fees to international consultants in 1983/84, amounting in some cases to as much as 15 per cent

of the total cost of the project - despite the fact that fees were being forced down far below official levels by shrewd clients all over the world.

22. See N. Lemunge, 'Management and Construction', paper presented to the CIB Congress, Oslo, 1980.

23. Suggestions along these lines were made by both the Ministry of Works, Local Construction Industry Study and the ILO/DFK draft report.

24. Construction activity in 1982 accounted for only 3.8 per cent of GDP, compared with 5.3 per cent in 1973, see United Republic of Tanzania, Economic Survey 1983.

25. It was a 'lack of political will and commitment' on the part of the Government of Ghana that was held by G. Ofori to be the major factor responsible for that country's failure to solve similar construction industry problems, see G. Ofori, 'The Construction Industries of Developing Countries: The Applicability of Existing Theories and Strategies for their Improvement and lessons for the Future: The Case of Ghana', unpublished Ph.D thesis, University of London, 1980.

Chapter Eight

CONCLUSIONS IN THE LIGHT OF THE DEVELOPMENT OF CONSTRUCTION RESOURCES IN CUBA

The last two chapters have examined government policies for the development of the construction industry in two neighbouring countries in East Africa, Kenya and Tanzania. Policies pursued appear to have been very different. Thus, in Kenya a policy of 'Africanisation' was adopted, whereby a conscious effort was directed towards the encouragement of African capital into the contracting industry, to supplement or replace Asian capital. The policy met with only limited success. After fifteen years and a great deal of investment in time and money a handful of African contractors had been carefully nurtured into category 'A' - heavily subsidised and protected against competition from established Asian firms.

Tanzania, on the other hand, has followed a policy of 'nationalisation', whereby the state took over a number of privately-owned assets and itself assumed the role of producer in the construction process. The motivation behind such action was to obtain for the state a share of the profits of the private contracting industry, as well as to increase competition in the construction industry by adding to the very limited contracting capacity existing in the private sector. Again, the policy met with only limited success. The state presence did create additional capacity in the industry, but this had only a marginal effect upon the level of competition and therefore upon prices and profits in the industry as a whole.

It may in fact be argued that the policies adopted by governments in Kenya and Tanzania were not really so very different. Both were policies of 'localisation'; or attempts to obtain some greater degree of local control over the process of production in an industry dominated by foreigners and other ethnic minorities, who appeared to be making excessive profits.

On the other hand, neither policy was really a response to the problems of the construction sector. Governments did not seriously consider the construction demands likely to arise during the process of the implementation of development plans, and the ability of the sector to respond. Advisers were indeed called in and their reports did illuminate serious bottlenecks and organisation flaws. But in both countries when it came to policy formulation such findings were largely ignored.

Furthermore, because the fundamental problems were not addressed, neither country - despite the rhetoric - actually adopted a radical policy. The structure of the construction industry was never challenged. Governments hoped simply to replace, or supplement, resources within the existing structure. Consequently, neither Kenya nor Tanzania really experimented with any different basis for the development of indigenous resources in the construction industry.

Before attempting to answer the question as to whether or not things might have been different, whether there were alternatives available to the governments of Kenya and Tanzania in the 1960s and 1970s for a remodelling of their construction sectors, it seems appropriate to pause and consider the experience of a third country where development of the construction sector has followed a very different trajectory. Much of this chapter will therefore be devoted to an analysis of the development of construction resources in Cuba.

THE HISTORY OF CONSTRUCTION IN CUBA

In pre-revolutionary Cuba more than 60 per cent of industry and services were located in Havana. The concentration of resources was even more marked in the construction sector, with 90 per cent of the architects and almost all of the large contractors (many of whom were American-owned or controlled) being based in the capital city. Construction demand in the monetary economy emanated largely from a wealthy minority. It was a demand for luxury houses, plush hotels and the inevitable commercial office blocks. Most people, whether landless labourers on the sugar plantations and big estates, or 'hangers-on' around the fringes of the urban economy, lived in poverty and squalor - their meagre demands for shelter being met largely within the 'informal' sector of the economy. In the absence of any kind of popular building programme, the existence of an abundant supply of cheap labour (due to the widespread occurrence of both cyclical and permanent unemployment) meant that the construction demand of the minority group could easily be met using traditional materials and techniques. If agriculture or industrial structures were required, then whole plants (as well as materials, equipment, contractors and skilled manpower) had to be imported, mostly from the United States. Thus, in some respects the situation in Cuba before the Revolution was similar to that pertaining in East Africa today - except that the demand for luxury buildings in the latter case emanates from the state and its institutions.

In the years immediately following the revolution of 1959, the vast majority of architects and engineers, as well as most of the large contractors, left the country. The assets they left behind were taken over by the state, or by various kinds of cooperative groups, and were soon put to use in a great surge of building activity. The immediate task was to clear the worst of the slums. Between 1959 and 1963 an average of 17,000 new housing units were built each year, by a combination of self-help groups, state construction brigades, and a few remaining private companies. The nationalisation of construction enterprises was not completed until 1968.[1]

Construction activity was soon affected however, along with many other sectors of the economy, by a mounting pressure against resources.[2] The U.S. trade embargo, imposed in 1962, meant that the traditional source of construction materials, components and equipment had been closed. Also, with the re-distribution of land in the countryside - people moved into more rewarding tasks in agriculture and industry and unemployment was quickly eliminated. The traditional surplus of labour for construction became a shortage. Thus, Cuba was faced with a severe shortage of construction materials and a dwindling supply of construction labour, at the same time as it was attempting to launch a broad-based development programme, under which the volume of construction work generated was likely to substantially increase. Cuba's answer to this dilemma was to embark upon a programme of investment for the domestic production of building materials, and to begin industrialisation of the construction sector.

CONCLUSIONS

The essential elements of the industrialisation of construction are the standardisation of building designs and the rationalisation of production techniques. The term frequently also implies the prefabrication of a substantial amount of the work previously carried out on the building site and the mechanisation of the remaining tasks. Thus, output can be substantially and rapidly increased with a less than proportionate increase in the labour force (although not necessarily a reduction in cost per unit). Before 1959, there were only two small prefabrication plants in Cuba, both in Havana. Between 1960 and 1962, two more small plants were built outside of Havana and three in the interior, all with Cuban technology. These early experiments with prefabrication showed the need to develop a long-term programme of applied research that would facilitate improvements in both design and building methods, using Cuban resources and adapted to Cuban conditions. Work groups were formed within the Ministry of Construction to look into modular coordination, standardisation of materials components and the development of model types for building designs. As the work advanced, new industrialised building systems were introduced. Most impressive of these is perhaps the 'Giron', named after 'Playa Giron', otherwise known as the 'Bay of Pigs'. It is an entirely Cuban system developed in the late 1960s for schools in the countryside, and used since for a number of purposes, including hotels. But undoubtedly the most interesting, as well as the most relevant to other developing countries, is the 'Sandino' system named after the Nicaraguan national hero. It consists of prefabricated concrete columns, beams, wall and roof panels, assembled with the help of a pulley system, and made with a technology so simple as to be considered almost a form of artisanry.[3] By 1980 there were a total of 128 prefabrication plants located throughout the country. All agricultural, industrial and social buildings are now prefabricated, as is also some housing. For a variety of reasons, however, some housing is still built with traditional construction techniques. But it is significant that even when this is the case, the principles of industrialisation - the standardisation of components, the simplification and repetition of design details and the rationalisation of construction methods using specialised building construction methods using specialised building brigades - are being very effectively employed.[4]

Parallel to the development of industrialised

building systems, Cuba launched a very extensive investment programme for the production of construction materials, which began to bear fruit in the 1970s. Cement is the key material in construction. As late as 1970, substantial quantities of this material were still being imported into Cuba from the USSR, France and West Germany. But domestic production increased by 40 per cent in 1971 and by 50 per cent in 1972, to reach a total of 2.6 million tons by 1976 - an increase of 260 per cent in just six years.[5] Production of cement has continued to rise, reaching 3.6 million tons by 1981 - a figure which places Cuba in line with the countries of Eastern Europe, and slightly ahead of the countries of Western Europe, in terms of cement production per head of population. In terms of other building materials, performance has also been fairly impressive. Factories have been established for the production of concrete products, asbestos-cement sheets, sanitary fixtures, glazed tiles and prefabricated systems, as well as the basic products such as sand, stone, bricks and blocks. Total output of all building materials together increased almost exactly four times in value between 1970 and 1980. Today, Cuba is self-sufficient in many of these products - although it is still necessary to import some of the raw material inputs, as well as specialised finishes and sophisticated electrical equipment such as lifts.

These investments in the building materials industries in the 1960s, together with the industrialisation of construction, laid the basis for the dramatic increase in construction output that was to follow. In 1958, the output of the construction industry was valued at 227 million pesos; in 1970 it was still only 436 million pesos. But from 1970 to 1981, construction output grew at an average rate of 14.2 per cent per annum.[6] So that by 1980 it was valued (in constant prices) at 1,536 million pesos - almost seven times the 1958 figure.[7] The work-force in construction in 1958 was only 83,000. By 1983 it had risen to 400,000, representing more than 15 per cent of the total employed labour force. Thus construction has become a major sector of the Cuban economy. It has even become a significant earner of foreign-exchange. In 1981, Cuban construction teams were working in Angola, Tanzania, Iraq, Libya and Ethiopia, as well as in a number of countries in Latin America.[8] Export earnings from overseas construction work amounted to approximately 30 million pesos per year.

CONCLUSIONS

THE COMPOSITON OF CONSTRUCTION OUTPUT

Activity in the construction sector reflects the particular strategy for development and the varied aspirations and priorities of a country's government. In Cuba, the priorities for construction investment to date have been the provision of basic infrastructure (ports, railways and roads); agricultural development schemes; industrial buildings; and, in the social field, investments in education and health. In these areas, the achievements have been impressive. Thus, between 1958 and 1975, electricity output increased three times; there were substantial improvements in port facilities; and a modern system of roads was created throughout the country. During the same period, the area of irrigated land increased fourfold, through the construction of dams, reservoirs and thousands of kilometres of irrigation canals.[9] Investments allocated to industrial projects increased from 480 million pesos during 1971-1975 to 1350 million pesos during the first Five-Year Plan (1976-1980). A number of new industrial plants were built such as sugar mills, textile plants, cement factories, a nickel refinery, and an integrated plant for the supply of agricultural equipment.[10] Finally, in the field of social investments, 970 new schools have been completed, as well as more than 1,000 'medical aid units' - ranging from first aid posts, through medical posts and polyclinics, to full-service hospitals.

Perhaps surprisingly, housing has not had high priority in Cuba's construction programme to date. Although the limited resources allocated to it have presumably been backed up by attention to use of the available stock, and by schemes to make the materials and skills stretch a bit, the output of houses (at about 20,000 per annum) still falls far short of the estimated need of 100,000 new units each year. With most of the demand for educational and social buildings now satisfied, it may be that higher priority will go to housing in the future. And there is no doubt that the development of indigenous construction resources places the country in a better position for tackling the housing shortage.

There are, however, two key constraints on the volume of new construction work. The first of these, ironically, is foreign exchange. For although most construction materials and components are now produced at home, some basic raw materials must be imported, as must the plant and equipment and the energy to run it. (Cuba has no energy resources of its own). Here one must be critical (as are many Cubans themselves) of the apparently increasing use of high-rise construction techniques, such as the imported Yugoslav 'IMS' system. They increase the demand for energy quite significantly, as well as for imported plant and equipment and specialised installations such as lifts. This dilemma may eventually be overcome by the development of the machinery industry for the production of construction plant and equipment in Cuba; efforts in this sector to date have concentrated upon the production of agricultural machinery, spare parts, buses and trucks. In the short-term, however, foreign-exchange could be saved through the more efficient use of plant and equipment and through the development of lighter systems of prefabrication. Cuba should also in the future make more extensive use of the one low-energy system it has already developed (the Sandino system), which is well-suited to the construction of one or two storey housing units, in urban or rural areas; and especially of rationalised and improved traditional construction techniques, such as those employed in the construction of large housing estates just outside Havana.

The second key constraint on the further expansion of construction output is the limited availability of construction labour. It is not possible to expand production by increasing the size of the labour force; increased output must come from higher output per worker. Further industrialisation and mechanisation of the construction process has limited potential. Productivity increases are now dependent upon improving efficiency - a particularly difficult problem in centrally-planned economies. Certain steps have already been taken towards this end, such as the centralisation of construction under one ministry; the inauguration of a system of project 'vetting' at the planning and design stage, so as to ensure greater economy in the use of resources; the introduction of a variety of incentives, both monetary and moral, individual and collective; and even the development of a new system of decentralised economic management, whereby all construction enterprises have to become self-accounting and performance is judged by the level of 'profits'. It is too early as yet to assess the effectiveness of these measures.[11]

Against the problem of resource constraints one must also evaluate the 'Microbrigade' experiment, devised in the early 1970s to accelerate the housing programme. A microbrigade is made up of 30 workers, temporarily detached from their work centres and regular assignments to work full-time in house construction, under the supervision of a few experienced builders. Workers remaining at the work centre make up for the loss of the microbrigade members by performing additional labour. In this way, many more houses have been constructed with no net addition to the workforce. The microbrigade programme also claims to have wider importance than the additional houses so constructed, in the sense of a presumed advance towards popular participation in decision-making and towards the 'socialisation' of the work process. Thus, through the creation of the microbrigades 'workers have been brought together in a situation where they must develop new leaders, make decisions about the hours and methods of their work, and bear direct responsibility for their actions. The continued reliance on this form of labour involves a continued training of workers in decision making processes.'[12] In addition, workers in the work centre from which the microbrigade force has been drawn are also obliged to focus attention upon organisation. At first they undertook voluntary overtime to make up the work; subsequently attention turned to productivity increases through better organisation. In this way, something of the order of 28,000 workers have presumably been shifted to construction without major repercussions on the level of output in other sectors. (Obviously the efficiency of running those sectors left something to be desired, but this book is not concerned with that). Finally, through the creation of microbrigades and other 'special programmes' it has been possible to integrate women into work previously thought of as men's preserve.[13] At their peak in 1973, microbrigades accounted for 65 per cent of all houses built in Cuba.[14] But the idea of relying on microbrigades to solve the housing deficit has since been challenged. Today opinion is divided. Many feel that the use of untrained labour results in low productivity and considerable wastage of material. Also, the limits to the process of squeezing out surplus, or underemployed, labour from other sectors of the economy may now have been reached. On the other hand, the social and political benefits of having workers participate in the production of their own houses can hardly be denied.

Chapter Eight

CUBAN EXPERIENCE : AN ASSESSMENT

It may be concluded that Cuba has achieved a significant transformation in its construction sector. It has exploited local materials resources and set up a whole range of both extractive and manufacturing building materials industries. It has trained a local labour force to perform all of the tasks involved in the construction process, from the design of the product right through to its final assembly. And it has developed its own industrialized building systems, based upon the repetition of standard design details, and the manufacture (on or off the building site) of standardised component parts. As a result, Cuba has been able to sustain a high level of domestic building activity, as well as to serve as a net exporter of building services. What is more, developments in the construction sector have contributed significantly to the structural transformation of the economy as a whole. In 1980 the Cuban economy, although still dependent on sugar, was far more industrialised and diversified than in 1960.[15]

What then accounts for Cuba's record in a field which, in many other countries, has lagged? How has this transformation been brought about? Are there lessons for other developing countries?

Cuban experience demonstrates what can be achieved when the process of design is brought under control, and both plans and products are standardised. Once this occurs then some types of prefabrication are no longer an impossible dream, even for countries at low levels of development. In this connection, a radical re-structuring of the relationships between the various participants in the construction process is helpful. In Cuba today, professional rivalries are less significant. Architects are now seen as part of the building team (perhaps even a subordinate part) rather than as experts of a superior status - as is demonstrated by the fact that they no longer supervise the construction process, but have only the exercise of 'author's rights' to ensure that the final construction product corresponds to the original design. At the same time, the practice of solving individual, isolated design cases has been rejected in favour of team work on the development of systems - or the search for a long-term solution to more general building problems. Finally, there have been many radical departures from the traditional educational approach - among them an experiment whereby architectural students spend one half of their time, during the first two years of study, actually working on a building site.[16] It seems that other developing countries wishing to use Cuba's experience in the construction field should pay attention to the development of the curricula in their schools of design, as well as to the way in which the work of architects and engineers is integrated into the total construction process.

In addition to changing the relationship between designers and producers in the construction industry, the rapid expansion of construction output through the use of industrialised processes may in Cuba have been promoted by some central direction and control over much of the construction programme. Is therefore some degree of central planning an essential precondition for the industrialisation of construction? Before reaching any firm conclusions on this issue, it may be worthwhile to consider the experience of a few European countries that have attempted to industrialise their construction sector.

Following the Second World War, the European region as a whole underwent a period of very rapid economic growth, accompanied by an even more rapid expansion of output from the construction sector. A shortage of labour resulting from the expansion of the economy in general, as well as a shortage of skilled labour in construction, pointed towards an 'industrial' solution to the construction problem. The countries of Eastern Europe, with planned economies 'have shown the ability to proceed easily to the creation of a new industry' and 'offered favourable conditions for the construction of large factories (for the production of buildings) with a high degree of mechanisation and automation'.[17] Some degree of industrialisation of the building process, particularly in housing, was also achieved in Western European countries. But in order for this to occur, strong government action was required. The situation is summarised in the following passage from the Economic Commission for Europe:

> In countries with a partly-planned or market economy, prefabrication by the state has not been adopted (though local councils have been known to build and operate prefabrication factories). However, fairly direct and stringent measure were taken by countries which most needed to industrialise. A classic

> measure is the 'launching' contract, of sufficient size to instigate the establishment of a factory. Another, somewhat less direct, measure may be called the 'reserved sector'; this involves the creation of a guaranteed volume of orders which is allocated to a given technology. An even simpler measure is to organise the market so that contracts will be of the size most advantageous for the industrialised technologies it is wished to promote. In all the market economy countries, the role of the public authorities has been to provide favourable conditions for setting-up the factories (or equipment) for industrialised building, while the investments as such have been financed by private means. The main aim of the measures taken by the authorities has been to ensure a minimum of continuity in the demand for the products. In the planned economies, the same objective is achieved through the state plans.[18]

Hence, 'under heavy demand pressure, the European construction industry tripled its output (measured in fixed prices) in less than two decades and underwent a technological and structural transformation, actively sponsored or strongly promoted by governments'.[19]

Further insights into the role of governments in promoting this transformation in Europe may be gleaned from the following:

> In the course of the efforts to 'industrialise' construction, it became increasingly clear that some of the main obstacles to improved efficiency in construction were not of a technical nature, but were to be found in the institutional and legislative framework governing construction activities. Thus, in all countries building laws and regulations were thoroughly revised, updated and - to a larger or lesser extent - unified. Standardisation of building products was promoted as a pre-requisite for a rational production and use of industrially-made components. Annual budgetary allocations for construction purposes were gradually replaced by longer-term financing schemes, or rolling plans. A better continuity of demand was also promoted by the stimulation of cooperation between clients with similar building programmes and by the unification, as far as possible, of users' requirements. Finally, the intricate and

controversial question of contracting procedures, especially for public expenditure, was subjected to careful scrutiny.[20]

Thus it appears that the rapid expansion of construction output through the industrialisation of the construction process can be achieved, even in market economies. As with other industries, the key to success lies in collective action (public if necessary) to promote the standardisation of construction designs; together with changes in planning and contract procedures to facilitate continuity of demand; and changes in institutions and legislation with respect to construction activity. The gains are such that in some countries strictly private cooperation has brought standardisation about - for example, the use of standard catalogues of construction components such as that published by McGraw Hill and widely used in the United States. In developing countries, however, we have already shown that the presence of an innovative private sector can by no means be taken for granted. Great initiative on the part of government may be required in order to propel faltering construction industries on to a new and more dynamic development path. Far from rolling back the frontiers of state intervention (as advocated, for example, by the World Bank) it would seem that in countries such as Kenya and Tanzania, the state must be prepared to experiment with a more active role in some parts of the construction sector.

It may of course be objected that the industrialisation of the construction process, such as has occurred in Cuba, is not and should not be the major aim of the majority of very poor countries. Premature adoption of industrialised construction methods may lead to higher costs of construction in developing countries, due to inadequate levels of demand and high costs of transport. It may also reduce the opportunities for the employment of local labour, while requiring larger amounts of both capital and foreign-exchange than more conventional construction techniques. Such arguments are undoubtedly valid. And they are strongly reinforced by the experiences of a number of poor countries that have experimented with imported industrial construction systems, whether they be from market or planned economies.[21] Interestingly, the export of Cuban construction systems to Africa would seem to prove no exception to this general pattern. In 1975, Cubans began construction of three secondary schools in Tanzania, using their Giron system. The technology employed seemed to be too sophisticated for Tanzanian conditions; training was inadequate; spare parts for the construction moulds were unobtainable; and although the three schools were completed, Tanzanians on their own were unable to complete a fourth.

It would, however, be wrong to conclude simply because imported systems have failed, that the industrialisation of the construction process is not relevant to countries at low levels of technological development. Industrialisation does not necessarily imply the production of a standard building - such as, for example, in a factory manufacturing large panels or concrete box units, known as the 'model' approach and widely used in Eastern Europe and the USSR. Neither does it necessarily imply the prefabrication of standard components according to a single system, such as adopted in Cuba. The term industrialisation may simply be used to indicate the rationalisation of production processes and techniques and the mass-production of component parts. Thus, it may be a particular manifestation of industrialisation that is inappropriate to African conditions, rather than the process *per se*. Whatever the level of technology adopted the basic principles behind any kind of industrial process are *standardisation* and *repetition*. The application of these principles to construction - in the planning and design of the product, in the use of technology and in the execution of the structure - *will* open the door to prefabrication, of complete facilities or components. But it will also greatly facilitate the economic production of a wide variety of traditional materials and industrial products - after all, even bricks and blocks can be mass-produced. It should also simplify training requirements and reduce the skills and experience required for construction supervision and management. Finally, it will drastically reduce the demand for professional manpower - and enable what is available to be used to maximum effect.

It seems probable that African countries, and others at very low levels of development, could make progress in this direction. Careful government action to secure a re-structuring of relationships in the construction sector, and to initiate the development and use of standard designs, could be the starting point. If such designs were to be based upon the repetition of a limited number of production and assembly operations on-site, incorporating locally-available materials and locally-produced components, this could lead to a breakthrough in productivity in the construction industry. In so far as it involves the greater use of domestic resources to satisfy domestic demand, it would also constitute a vital step in the 'inward-reorientation' of the economy - seen by a number of authors as an essential precondition for raising the level of development of small, dependent, underdeveloped economies.[22] Thus it is conceivable that changes in the construction sector could play a major role in the diversification and industrialisation of African economies, as has happened in Cuba. But positive action will be required to achieve this end.

NOTES

1. See E. Boorstein, The Economic Transformation of Cuba (Monthly Review Press, New York, 1968).
2. Ibid.
3. A full description of this system can be found in J.K. Black et al. Area Handbook for Cuba, second edition (US Government Printing Office, Washington, 1976).
4. See Comite Estatal de la Construccion, Arquitectura y Desarollo Nacional, Cuba (CEDITEC, Havana, 1978).
5. These and other statistics in this section are taken from Annuario Estadistico de Cuba, Havana (various dates).
6. C. Brundenius, Revolutionary Cuba : The Challenge of Economic Growth with Equity (Westview Press, Boulder and London, 1984).
7. See United Nations Comision para America Latina (CEPAL), Cuba : Notas par el Estudio Economico de America Latina (CEPAL, Mexico, 1980).
8. Granma Weekly Review, April 19, 1981. For further details of overseas construction operations see also Granma, August 29, 1976/January 9, 1977/ May 20, 1979/April 12, 1981.
9. Comite Estatal de la Construccion, Arquitectura y Desarollo.
10. Brundenius, Revolutionary Cuba, p.67.
11. I am grateful to the Ministerio de la Construccion in Havana for the information contained in this paragraph.
12. See A. MacEwan, Revolution and Economic Development in Cuba (Macmillan, London, 1980).
13. Ibid.

14. R. Mace, 'Housing' in Griffiths, J. and Griffiths, P. (Eds.). Cuba: The Second Decade (Writers and Readers, London, 1979).

15. Brundenius, Revolutionary Cuba, p.119.

16. T. Schuman, 'We Don't Have the Right to Wait', Cuba Review, vol. 5, no. 1 (Cuba Resource Centre, New York, 1975); and S. Torre, 'Architecture and Revolution in Cuba: 1959 to 1974' Progressive Architecture (New York, 1974).

17. United Nations Economic Commission for Europe (UN/ECE), Human Settlements in Europe: Post-War Trends and Policies (UN/ECE/HBP/18, 1976), pp. 93 & 88.

18. Ibid., pp. 88-89.

19. Ibid., p.91.

20. United Nations Economic Commission for Europe (UC/ECE), Structural Trends in European Manufacturing Output and Trade (E/ECE/814, 1976).

21. For a history of such failure see W.P. Strassmann, Housing and Building Technology in Developing Countries (Michigan State University, 1978).

22. See, for example, C. Thomas, Dependence and Transformation : The Economics of the Transition to Socialism (Monthly Review Press, 1974); and G. Tolnai, The Growth of Big Industry and the Domestic Market in the Third World (Budapest, 1980).

BIBLIOGRAPHY

Aldington, T. et. al. 'The Economics of Kenyanisation', East Africa Journal, vol. V, no. 3 (1968).

Andrews, J. et. al. Construction and Development: a Framework for Research and Action (Building Economics Research Group, University College London, 1972).

Annuario Estadistico de Cuba, Havana - various dates.

Balkenhol, B. 'Small Contractors: Untapped Potential or Economic Impediment? Some Observations on the Construction Industry in Cameroon, Niger and Sierra Leone', World Employment Programme Research Working Paper WEP 2-22/WP.48 (International Labour Office, Geneva, 1979).

Banco Nacional de Cuba, Economic Report (Havana, August 1982).

Banwell, H. The Placing and Management of Contracts for Building and Civil-Engineering Works (HMSO, London, 1964).

Barker and Barton, 'The Construction Industry in Tanzania: The Current situation: November 1980', Barker and Barton (Tanzania) Ltd., 1980.

Barton, B. 'The Construction Industry in Tanzania: The Current Situation', Quantity Surveyor, no. 38 (July 1982).

Berliner, J.S. The USSR Construction Industry (Council for Economic and Industry Research, Washington, 1955).

Bhalla, A.S. 'Technological Choice in Construction in Two Asian Countries: China and India', World Development vol. 2 no. 3 (1974).

Bienefeld, M.A. 'The Construction Industry in Tanzania', Economic Research Bureau Paper no. 69.4 (University of Dar-Es-Salaam, 1969).

Black, J.K. et. al. Area Handbook for Cuba, second edition (US Government Printing Office, Washington, 1976).

Boorstein, E. The Economic Transformation of Cuba (Monthly Review Press, New York, 1968).

Bowen, I. 'The Case for Rationalisation of the Building Industry', Manchester School of Economic and Social Studies Vol. 19, no. 2 (1951).

Bowley, M. The British Building Industry: Four Studies in Response and Resistance to Change (Cambridge University Press, 1966).

Bromley, R. (ed.). The Urban Informal Sector: Critical Perspectives on Employment and Housing Policies (Pergamon Press, Oxford, 1979).

BIBLIOGRAPHY

Brundenius, C. Revolutionary Cuba: The Challenge of Economic Growth with Equity (Westview Press, Boulder and London, 1984).

Building Research Unit, 'Building Cost Indices', Working Report no. 28 (Building Research Unit, Dar-Es-Salaam, 1982).

Burgess, R. in Bromley, R. (ed.). The Urban Informal Sector: Critical Perspectives on Employment and Housing Policies (Pergamon Press, Oxford, 1979).

Burgess, D. 'A Study of the Construction Industry in Tanzania', Ministry of Economic affairs and Development Planning, Dar-Es-Salaam, 1971.

Campbell, P.A. 'Legal Economic and Technical Problems in the Establishment of Construction Industries in Developing Countries, with Particular Reference to Kenya', Technical Meeting on The Construction Industry in Developing Countries ID/WG.148/8 (UNIDO, Vienna, 1973).

Capt. J. & Edmonds, G.A. 'Study of Small Contractors in Kenya' World Employment Programme Research Working Paper, WEP 2-22/WP 33 (International Labour Office, Geneva, 1977).

Cockburn, C. 'Construction: A Management Problem', Architects Journal (15 October, 1969).

—— Construction in Overseas Development: A Search for Appropriate Aid and Trade Measures for the 1970s (Overseas Development Institute, London, 1970).

—— 'Nigerian Building Contractors: Practices, Problems and Needs', Building for Development Research Paper no. 1 (Building for Development, London, 1970).

Comite Estatal de la Construccion, Arquitectura y Desarollo Nacional, Cuba (CEDITEC, Havana, 1978).

Coulson, A. 'Blood-Sucking Contracts' in Mapulo, H. (ed.) Workers and Management (Tanzania Publishing House, 1976).

—— Tanzania: A Political Economy (Clarendon Press, Oxford, 1982.

Cuba Review (Cuba Resource Centre, New York) - various issues.

Direct Labour Collective, Building with Direct Labour (Housing Workshop of the Conference of Socialist Economists, London, 1978).

Drewer, S. 'In Search of a Paradigm - Notes on the work of D.A. Turin', Habitat International Vol. 3 no. 1/2 (1978).

—— 'Traditional Industries in Modern Capitalist Economies: The Construction Sector in France and the U.K.' Unpublished Ph.D thesis, University of Sussex, 1979.

—— 'The Role of Construction in the National Economies' study for the UN/ECE,(1980).

—— 'Construction and Development: A New Perspective', Habitat International Vol. 5 no. 3/4 (1980).

Dyker, D.K. The Process of Investment in the Soviet Union (Cambridge University Press, 1983).

Edmonds, G.A. 'The Construction Industry in Developing Countries', International Labour Review Vol. 118 no. 3 (1979).

—— & Miles, D.W.J. Foundations for Change: Aspects of the Construction Industry in Developing Countries (Intermediate Technology Publications, London, 1984).

Emmerson, H. Survey of Problems before the Construction Industries, report prepared for the Ministry of Works (HMSO, London, 1962).

Freeman, I.L. 'Comparative Studies of the Construction Industries in Great Britain and North America: A Review', Building Research Establishment Current Paper CP5/81 (Building Research Establishment 1981).

Ganeson, S. 'Employment Generation through Investment in Housing and Construction', unpublished Ph.D thesis, University of London, 1976.

—— 'The Construction Industry in Sri-Lanka', World Employment Programme Research Working Paper WEP 2-22/WP.90 (International Labour Office, Geneva, 1982).

—— The Management of Small Construction Firms. Case Studies of Sri-Lanka, Singapore, Hong-Kong, Thailand, Philippines and Japan (Asian Productivity Organisation, Tokyo, 1982).

Germidus, D.A. The Construction Industry in Mexico (OECD Development Centre, Paris, 1972).

Ghai, D., Godfrey, M. & Lisk, F. Planning for Basic Needs in Kenya: Performance, Policies and Prospects (International Labour Office, Geneva, 1979).

Gorynski, J. 'The Role of Construction in Global Socio-Economic Development', Habitat International vol. 3 no. 1/2 (1978).

—— & Piatek, S. 'The Construction Industry in Poland', International Institute for Labour Studies Research Series no. 64 (Geneva, 1981).

Granma, Official Newspaper of the Communist Party of Cuba - various dates.

Grant, S.A. (ed.). Soviet Housing and Urban Design (U.S. Department of Housing and Urban Development, Washington, 1980).

Gray, C. & Flanagan, R. 'US Productivity and Fast-Tracking Start on the Drawing Board', Construction Management and Economics no. 2 (1984) pp.133-143.

Grimson, M. in Building Design no. 524 (December 1980).

Groak, S. 'Economic Theories of Building: a Basis for Criticism', unpublished M.Sc report, University College London, 1972.

Hardoy, J. & Acosta, M. 'Urbanisation Policies in Revolutionary Cuba' in Hardoy and Giesse (eds.) Latin American Urban Research Vol. 2 (Sage Publications, 1972).

Hardoy, J. 'The Recommendations of the U.N. Conference on Human Settlements and their Viability in Latin America', Habitat International vol. 3 no. 1/2 (1978).

Hayuma, A.M. 'Dodoma: The Planning and Building of the New Capital City of Tanzania', Habitat International vol. 5 no. 5/6 (1981).

Higgin, G. & Jessop, N. Communications in the Building Industry: Report of a Pilot Study (Tavistock Publications, London, 1965).

Hill, B.J. 'Why Construction is Quicker and Cheaper in theUSA', Chartered Surveyor no. 112 (1979), pp.158-161.

Hillebrandt, P.M. Economic Theory and the Construc-Industry (Macmillan, London, 1974).

Howard, M.D. & Howard, J.R. 'Cuba's New Towns', Urban Design, vol. 8, no. 2 (1977).

Hutton, J. 'Building and Construction in Papua-New Guinea's Development: a Survey of Problems and Prospects', Economic Development Research Project, Paper no. 168 (Makerere Institute of Social Research, Uganda, 1968).

International Bank for Reconstruction and Development (IBRD), 'Study of the Substitution of Labour and Equipment in Civil-Construction' Staff Working Paper no. 172 (1974).

—— 'A Framework for the Promotion of Construction Industries in Developing Countries', Staff Working Paper no. 168 (1973).

—— /World Bank, The Construction Industry: Issues and Strategies in Developing Countries (The World Bank, Washington, 1984).

BIBLIOGRAPHY

International Labour Office (ILO), 'Technological changes in the Construction Industry and their Socio-Economic Consequences', Seventh Session of the Building, Engineering and Public Works Committee (ILO, Geneva, 1964).

—— 'Social Aspects of Prefabrication in the Construction Industry', Report II of the Eighth Session of the Building, Engineering and Public Works Committee (ILO, Geneva, 1968).

—— 'Social Problems in the Construction Industry arising out of the Industrialisation of Developing Countries', Report III of the Eighth Session of the Building, Engineering and Public Works Committee (ILO, Geneva, 1968).

—— 'Construction Skills', CIRF Monograph no. 4 (ILO, Geneva, 1969).

—— Employment, Incomes and Equality: a Strategy for Increasing Productive Employment in Kenya (ILO, Geneva, 1972).

—— World Employment Programme: Research in Retrospect and Prospect. (ILO, Geneva, 1976).

—— 'Building Rural Health Centres in Tanzania', Construction Management Programme Case Study (ILO, Geneva, 1980).

ILO/DFK, draft report of an ILO Mission to Tanzania to advise on contractor support, October, 1983.

Ive, G. 'The Role of the Public Client in Building Production', in Proceedings of the Bartlett Summer School (University College London, 1980).

—— 'The Changing Interface between the Construction Industry and the Building Materials Industry in Britain: Hypothesis and Examples", in Proceedings of the Bartlett Summer School, 1982 (University College London, 1982).

Jaycox, E.V.K. & Hardy, C. 'Domestic Construction Industries in Developing Countries', Finance and Development vol. 12 no. 1(1975).

Kafandaris, S. 'The Building Industry in the Context of Development', Habitat International vol. 5 no. 3/4 (1980).

Kang Chao, The Construction Industry in Communist China (Edinburgh University Press, 1968).

Kaplan, N. A Comparison of Construction Costs in the USSR and the US (The Rand Corporation, Santa Monica, California, 1957).

King, K. The African Artisan: Education and the Informal Sector in Kenya (Heinemann, 1977).

Kitching, G.N. Class and Economic Change in Kenya: The Making of an African Petite-Bourgeoisie 1905-1970 (Yale University Press, 1980).

Koenigsberger, O.H. & Groak, S. (eds.). Essays in Memory of Duccio Turin:1926-1976 (Pergamon Press, Oxford, 1978).

Lemunge, N. 'The Experience of Public Construction in Tanzania', paper presented at a seminar on the Tanzanian construction industry, Dar-Es-Salaam, 1977.

—— 'Management and Construction', paper presented to the CIB Congress, Oslo, 1980.

Leys, C. Underdevelopment in Kenya : The Political Economy of Neocolonialism, 1964-1971 (Heinemann, London, 1975).

Mace, R. 'Housing' in Griffiths, J. & Griffiths, P. (eds.), Cuba : the Second Decade (Writers and Readers, London, 1979).

MacEwan, A. Revolution and Economic Development in Cuba (Macmillan, London, 1980).

Maynard Lovell, S. 'The Advantages of Direct Labour', Building (May, 1969).

McGee, T.G. 'Conservation and Dissolution in the Third World City: the Shanty Town as an element of Conservation', paper prepared for the Burg Wartenstein Symposium no. 73, New York, 1977.

—— The Urbanisation Process in the Third World (G. Bell & Son, London, 1980).

MECCO, 'MECCO Development Project 1981-1983', Ministry of Foreign Affairs, Helsinki.

Mesa Lago, C. 'Availability and Reliability of Statistics in Socialist Cuba', Latin American Research Review vol. 4 no. 1 & vol. 4 no. 2 (1969).

—— (ed.) Revolutionary Change in Cuba (Pittsburgh, 1971).

—— The Economy of Socialist Cuba: A Two-Decade Appraisal (Alberquerque, 1981).

Ministry of Works, Tanzania. Local Construction Industry Study (MOW, Dar-Es-Salaam, 1977).

—— 'Construction Projects for all Ministries and Parastatals', memo from the Principle Secretary, MOW, to all other Principle Secretaries, Heads of Departments, Heads of Parastatals, and Regional Development Directors (10/10/83).

Moavenzadeh, F. 'The Role of the Construction Industry in the Development Process', Public Policy vol. 22 no. 22 (1974).

—— 'Construction Industry in Developing Countries', World Development vol. 6 no. 1 (1978).

—— 'The Role and Contribution of the Construction Industry in Socio-Economic Growth in Developing Countries', report prepared for UNCHS, 1980.

Moavenzadeh, F. & Rossow, J.A.K. The Construction Industry in Developing Countries (Massachusetts Institute of Technology, 1975).

Moser, C.O.N. 'The Informal Sector or Petty Commodity Production: Autonomy or Dependence in Urban Development', Developing Planning Unit Working Paper no. 3 (University College London, 1978).

—— 'The Informal Sector Reworked : Viability and Vulnerability in Urban Development', paper presented at a UNCRD seminar in West Berlin, November 1983.

Mtui, A.L. 'The Exploitation, Use and Development of Indigenous Building Materials in Tanzania' in Seminar on Building Materials (National Construction Council, Dar-Es-Salaam, 1982).

Muench, L.H. 'A Final Demand Approach to the Informal Sector and Implications for Public Policies' in The Urban Informal Sector in Kenya, Occasional Paper no. 25 (Institute for Development Studies, Nairobi, 1977).

National Board for Prices and Incomes, Report on Architectural Costs and Fees, Cmnd. 3653 (HMSO, London, 1968).

National Construction Council, Tanzania, Seminar on on Building Materials (NCC, Dar-Es-Salaam, 1982).

—— Seminar on the Role of Contractors in National Development (NCC, Dar-Es-Salaam, 1982).

—— Architects' Role in the Construction Industry (NCC, Dar-Es-Salaam, 1983).

—— Role of Consulting Engineers in the Construction Industry (NCC, Dar-Es-Salaam, 1983).

National Economic Development Office (NEDO), Contracting in Civil-Engineering since Banwell (HMSO, London, 1968).

—— The Public Client and the Construction Industries (HMSO, London, 1975).

National Institute of Productivity, Tanzania. Development of UJENZI Corporation Soles, report for the Principle Secretary of the Ministry of Works (National Institute of Productivity, Dar-Es-Salaam, 1980).

Neo, R.B. International Construction Contracting (Gower Press, 1976).

Neumann, R. 'An Economic Analysis of the Past Ten Years' Struggle for Progress and Self-Reliance', Project Report no. 31: Housing and Construction in the Tanzanian Economy (Ministry of Lands, Housing and Dar-Es-Salaam, 1978).

Nigerian Economic Society, The Construction Industry in Nigeria (University of Ibadan, 1974).

Nyerere, J.K. The Arusha Declaration (TANU, Dar-Es-Salaam, 1967).

Ofori, G. 'The Construction Industries of Developing Countries: The Applicability of Existing Theories and Strategies for Their Improvement and Lessons for the Future: The Case of Ghana', unpublished Ph.D thesis, University of London, 1980.

—— 'Construction Industry in Ghana', World Employment Programme Research Working Paper WEP2-22/WP.73 (International Labour Office, Geneva, 1980).

Omarov, A.M. Organisation of Industry and Construction (Progress Publishers, Moscow, 1965).

Parsons-Fox, L. Building Construction as an Engine of Economic Growth: an Evaluation. (University of North Carolina, 1976).

Peattie, L.R. 'Some Second Thoughts on Site and Services', Habitat International, vol. 6. no. 1/2 (1982).

Relf, C. Helping Towards Self-Reliance: An Analysis of Government-Sponsored Assistance to Small-Scale Contacting Enterprises in Kenya, Swaziland and Botswana (International Labour Office, Geneva, 1981).

Republic of Kenya, Economic Survey (Government Printer, Nairobi, 1969).

—— National Construction Corporation Act (Government Printer, Nairobi, 1972).

—— Fourth Five-Year Development Plan, 1979-1983. (Government Printer, Nairobi, 1979).

—— Statistical Abstract (Government Printer, Nairobi, 1983 and 1984).

Rosenburg, N. Economic Planning in the British Building Industry: 1945-1949 (University of Pennsylvania Press, Philadelphia, 1960).

Rothaus, E. 'Cuba's Microbrigades', Urban Design, vol. 8 no. 2 (1977).

Royal Institute of Chartered Surveyors (RICS), U.K. and its Construction Industries. A Comparison of Design and Contract Procedures (RICS, 1979).

Rweyemamu, J. Underdevelopment and Industrialisation in Tanzania: A Study of Perverse Capitalist Development (Oxford University Press, 1973).

Schuman, T. 'We Don't Have the Right to Wait', Cuba Review, vol. 5 no. 1 (Cuba Resources Centre, New York, 1975).

Seers, D. (ed.) Cuba: The Economic and Social Revolution (University of North Carolina Press, 1964.)

Shrivastav, P.P. 'City for the Citizens or Citizens for the City', Habitat International, vol. 6 no. 1/2 (1982).

Siebolds, P. and Steinberg, F. 'Dodoma: A Future African Brazilia?', Habitat International, vol. 5, no. 5/6 (1980).

Stone, P.A. Building Economy: Design, Production, Organisation: A Synoptic View (Pergamon Press, Oxford, 1966).

Strassmann, W.P. 'Construction, Productivity and Employment in Developing Countries', International Labour Review, vol. 101 no. 5, 1970.

—— 'The Construction Sector in Economic Development', Scottish Journal of Political Economy, no. 17 (1970).

—— 'Building Technology and Employment in the Housing Sector of Developing Countries" World Employment Programme Research Working Paper WEP 2-22 (International Labour Office, Geneva, 1975).

—— Housing and Building Technology in Developing Countries (Michigan State University, 1978).

Stretton, A. 'The Building Industry and Employment Creation in Manila, the Philippines', unpublished Ph.D thesis, Australian National University, 1977.

—— 'The Building Industry in Papua-New Guinea', unpublished mimeo, 1979.

Sutcliffe, R.B. Industry and Underdevelopment (Addison-Wesley Publishing Co., 1971).

Swainson, N. The Development of Corporate Capitalism in Kenya: 1918-1977 (Heinemann, 1980).

SWECO, 'Review of NEDCO', report by a Swedish firm, Dar-Es-Salaam, 1980.

Swedish Ministry of Housing & Physical Planning, 'Swedish Assistance to Human Settlements in Tanzania - A Feasibility Study', 1982.

Tavistock Institute, Interdependence and Uncertainty (Tavistock Publications, 1966).

Thomas, C. Dependence and Transformation: The Economics of the Transition to Socialism (Monthly Review Press, 1974).

TISCO, Building Costs of Industrial Projects, study for the Ministry of Industry. (TISCO, Dar-Es-Salaam, 1978).

Tolnai, G. The Growth of Big Industry and the Domestic Market in the Third World (Budapest, 1980).

Torre, S. 'Architecture and Revolution in Cuba: 1959 to 1974', Progressive Architecture, New York (1974).

Turin, D.A. 'Some Hard Facts on the Economics of Building Industrialisation', Architects Journal 24th June (1964).

—— 'What do we Mean by Building', reprinted in Habitat International, vol. 5, no. 3/4 (1980).

—— Building as a Process (University College Environmental Research Group, University College London, 1967).

—— The Construction Industry: Its Economic Significance and its Role in Development (University College London, 1969) - also published as UNIDO Monograph on Industrial Development, no. 2.

—— Construction and Development (University College London, 1973).

—— 'The Role of Construction in Development Strategies', International Development Review, vol. XVL no. 3 (1974).

—— (ed.). Aspects of the Economics of Construction (George Godwin, 1975).

Turner, J.F.C. & Fichter, R. (ed.). Freedom to Build: Dweller Control of the Housing Process (Macmillan, London, 1972).

Turner, J.F.C. Housing by People (Marion Boyars, London, 1976).

United Nations Centre for Housing, Building and Planning (UNCHBP), 'Industrialisation of Building', Report by the Secretariat, Esosoc., to the Third Session of the Committee on Housing, Building and Planning, E/C.6/35, 1965.

—— 'Industrialisation of Building', Progress Report of the Centre for Housing, Building and Planning, E/C.6/52, 1966.

—— 'Industrialisation of the Building Industry' Progress Report of the Secretary-General on the Activities of the Centre for Housing Building and Planning, E/C.6/70/Add 1., 1967.

—— 'Research and Development Projects for Detailed Discussion: Building Technologies for Developing Countries', Report of the Secretary-General to the Eighth Session of the Committee on Housing, Building and Planning, E/C.6/137, 1973.

United Nations Centre for Human Settlements (UNCHS), 'Review of the Role and Contribution of the Construction Industry in Human Settlements Programmes and National Economic and Social Development', Report of the Executive Director of UNCHS to the Fourth Session of the Commission on Human Settlements, HS/C/4/3, 1981.

—— Government Policy Guidelines to Improve the Efficiency of the Construction Industry, HS/39/84/E (UNCHS, Nairobi, 1984).

United Nations Comision para America Latina (CEPAL), Appreciones Sobre el Estilo de Desarrollo y Sobre las Principales Politicas Sociales on Cuba, CEPAL/MEX/77/22/Rev.4 (1979).

—— Cuba: Notas para el Estudio Economico de America Latina, CEPAL/MEX/1017/Rev. 1 (1978); CEPAL/MEX/1030/Rev. 1 (1979); CEPAL/MEX/1044 (1980).

United Nations Department of Economic and Social Affairs, 'Construction Statistics', Studies in Methods, Series F, no. 13, 1965.

—— Trends in the Industrialization of Building, ST/SOA/102 (New York, 1970).

—— Guidelines for Government Policies and Measures for the Gradual Industrialisation of Building, ST/ESA/7 (New York 1974).

United Nations Economic Commission for Africa (UN/ECA), Housing in Africa, E/CN.14/HOU/7/Rev. 1 (1965).

—— Guide for the Building Industry in Africa, E/CN.14/HOU/91 (1971).

—— Prefabrication in Africa: Status and Problems, E/CN.14/HOU/101 (1973).

—— The Status and Problems of Housing and Construction Industry in Africa, E/CN.14/HOU/104 (1973).

—— Development of the Building Materials and Construction Industries in the United Republic of Tanzania (Addis Abbaba, 1983).

United Nations Economic Commission for Europe (UN/ECE), Cost, Repetition, Maintenance: Related Aspects of Building Prices ST/ECE/HOU/7 (1963).

—— Proceedings of the Seminar on Changes in the Structure of the Construction Industry needed to Improve its Efficiency and Increase its Output, Prague, (3 vols), ST/ECE/HOU/13 (1964).

—— Proceedings of the Second Seminar on the Building Industry, Paris (2 vols.), ST/ECE/HOU/36 (1967).

—— 'Development of the Building Materials and Components Sector', Report prepared by the ECE for the World Symposium on Industrial Development, Athens, mimeo, (1967).

—— Proceedings of the Third Seminar on the Building Industry, Moscow (2 vols.), ST/ECE/HOU/42 (1970).

—— Proceedings of the Fourth Seminar on the Building Industry, London, HBP/SEM. 3/3 (1973).

—— Human Settlements in Europe:Post-War Trends and Policies (ECE/HBP/18 (1976).

—— Long-Term Prospects and Policies in the Construction Sector, ECD/HBP/14 (1976).

—— Structural Trends in European Manufacturing Output and Trade (E/ECE/814 (1976).

United Nations Development Programme/International Labour Office (UNDP/ILO), 'The Labour-Intensive Special Works Programme in Tanzania', UNDP/ILO Project URT/77/033 (Prime Minister's Office, Dar-Es-Salaam, 1983).

United Nations Industrial Development Organisation (UNIDO), 'Construction Industry', Monographs On Industrial Development no. 2, ID/40/2 (New York, 1969).

—— Building Materials Industries: Factors affecting their Growth in Developing Countries (New York, 1969).

—— The Construction Industry in Developing Countries, Report of an Expert Group Meeting, Vienna, ID/WG.148/1-15 (1973).

—— Industrial Construction in Developing Countries, Report of an Expert Group Meeting, Vienna, ID/WG.169.9 (1974).

—— 'Appropriate Technology for Construction and Building Materials', Monographs on Appropriate Technology no. 12, ID/232/12 (1980).

United Republic of Tanzania, Economic Survey (Government Printer, Dar-Es-Salaam, 1982, 1983).

—— Ministry of Lands, Housing and Urban Development, Towards a National Housing Policy, report on a conference held in Arusha (1980).

—— Ministry of Planning and Economic Affairs, Structural Adjustment Programme for Tanzania (Dar-Es-Salaam, 1982).

Vitelli, G. 'Background Information on the Construction Industry and its Contribution to Human Settlements Programmes in Latin America', unpublished report prepared for the UNCHS, 1980.

Vevstad, F. 'National Construction Corporation of Kenya: an Approach to the Development of an Indigenous Construction Industry', Construction Management Programme: Case no. 1. (International Labour Office, Geneva, 1979).

Waterston, A. Development Planning: Lessons of Experience (John Hopkins, 1968).

Wells, E.J. & Rado, E.R. 'Constraints and Costs in the Kenya Building Industry', Staff Paper no. 22 (Institute for Development Studies, University of Nairobi, 1968).

Wells, E.J. 'The Production and Marketing of Ballast in Kenya', Miscellaneous Paper no. 8 (Institute for Development Studies, University of Nairobi, 1969).

—— 'The Construction Industry in East Africa', Economic Research Bureau Paper no. 72.2. (University of Dar-Es-Salaam, 1972).

—— 'The Structure of the Building Industry: Institutional and Administrative Changes Required for the Adoption of Appropriate Building Technology', paper presented to an ad hoc Expert Group Meeting of the UNCHBP, Amman, Jordan, 1977.

—— Expansion of Public-Sector Construction in Tanzania (National Construction Council, Dar-Es-Salaam, 1984).

—— 'The Small-Scale Production of Indigenous Building Materials in Developing Countries', unpublished report prepared for UNCHS, 1984.

—— 'The Construction Industry in the Context of Development: A New Perspective', Habitat International, vol. 8 no. 3/4 (1984).

—— 'The Role of Construction in Economic Growth and Development', Habitat International, vol. 9 no. 1 (1985).

Wheeler, M. 'Professional Fees of Design Consultants in the Kenya Building Industry East African Economic Review (December, 1969).

Index

Index

Index

Index

www.ingramcontent.com/pod-product-compliance
Lightning Source LLC
LaVergne TN
LVHW010628300926
849162LV00001B/95
9781041297253